DISCARD

The

Over- and

Bureau of
TEACHERS COLLEGE

Concepts of

Underachievement

ROBERT L. THORNDIKE

Teachers College, Columbia University

Publications (📖) 1963

COLUMBIA UNIVERSITY   NEW YORK

The Concepts of
Over- and Underachievement

60,822

ACKNOWLEDGEMENT

The research reported herein was supported through the
Cooperative Research Program of the Office of Education,
U. S. Department of Health, Education, and Welfare.

Contents

The Concepts of
Over- and Underachievement

1

Designing Research to Study
Achievement vs. Predicted Achievement

This monograph is written for educators who have become interested in "overachievement" and "underachievement" and who are considering setting up a research study to add to the already considerable body of literature in this somewhat tricky research area. (It should also be useful to those wishing to evaluate previous research with a view to using the findings in some way.) Unfortunately, much previous research is faulty in one or another aspect of its design. Much of what appears in the research literature is inconclusive, and some of it is downright misleading. This arises in part from defective experimental planning, and in part from inherent deficiencies in the terms "overachievement" and "underachievement" that are used to denote the problem. This monograph will examine these concepts, to see whether they have any value and perhaps to suggest alternatives for them, will point out some of the methodological problems and some of the errors to be avoided, and will suggest precautions to be observed if one is to obtain sound and meaningful results. Hopefully, it will lead to fewer and better publications in the future.

"OVERACHIEVEMENT" AND "UNDERACHIEVEMENT"
AS PSYCHOLOGICAL CONCEPTS

The first step in planning to do research on so-called "overachievement" and "underachievement" is to clarify one's own understanding of what the terms mean. Vague or faulty concepts have been the source of the faults in many past studies.

It seems obvious that we can only have "underachievement" in relation to some standard of expected or predicted achievement. So perhaps we should begin by asking where that standard of expected achievement comes from. We shall need to have a firm grasp of this standard of expected performance if we are to comprehend the research problems involved in studying deviations from it.

The simplest standard for expected performance is to expect that everyone will perform at the same level, i.e., that all human beings will be able to lift the same weight, tote the same bale, run at the same speed, do the same arithmetic problems, read the same literature. That is, we predict that each person will do no better and no worse than anyone else.

But as soon as we know anything at all about people, we know that this state of affairs does not hold. We soon come to know that in general men can lift more than women, 12-year-olds more than 10-year-olds, big 12-year-olds more than little 12-year-olds, and so forth. We learn that there are a whole series of facts that can be known about an individual that permit us to temper our expectations and make them more accurate. We learn that the more of the relevant facts we take into account, the more accurate our predictions or expectations can be. And we also learn that no matter how many related facts we have available, our predictions can never be exactly correct for every person. Even among 12-year-old farm boys weighing exactly 110 pounds, there is still a good deal of variation in how much they can lift. Moving to the domain of educational achievement, among 12-year-old farm boys with an IQ of 110, there is still a good deal of variation in how many words they can spell correctly or how many addition problems they can do in five minutes.

So "underachievement" and "overachievement" really refer to the imperfectness of our predictions. They refer to the fact that a group of pupils all of the same age, the same IQ, the same type of home background, will *still* vary in the scores that they obtain on a reading test or an arithmetic test, in the grades they receive from their science teacher or their history teacher. Our problem is to try to understand how and why these differences arise and to determine how those who achieve less well can be brought to achieve better. As a research problem, the problem of "underachievement" is one of understanding our failures in predicting achievement and of identifying more crucial factors or additional factors that will permit us to predict it more accurately. The research problem includes also the attempt to identify and manipulate the controllable factors influencing achievement, so that the level of achievement, especially of those doing less than we would expect them to, may be raised.

In much of the work on prediction of academic achievement, educators (and psychologists) have suffered from a kind of single-minded obsession with intelligence or scholastic aptitude tests as predictors. These tests have at times been virtually deified as an exemplification of exact and absolute truth. And it has been assumed that achievement somehow *ought* to correspond exactly to the level of performance on the aptitude test. There has been a feeling that things were somehow wrong if the correspondence was not maintained. There has been a tendency to forget that the aptitude test is, after all, only one sample of behavior from which another, usually somewhat larger and somewhat different sample is being forecast. It is important to put the scholastic aptitude test in proper perspective as just another test, just another sample of behavior, just another predictor. There is no more a priori justification for expecting an exact correspondence of academic achievement with a scholastic aptitude measure than there is to expect a perfect correspondence between height and age.

If we recognize that the prediction of academic achievement is just one example of the general problem of prediction, and that labelling a test a "scholastic aptitude test" confers no special status upon it, then we can approach the problem of "underachievement" as an example of the general phenomenon of errors of prediction or failure to predict. We can ask the perfectly general question: Why do we fail to achieve perfection in our attempts to predict? Answering the question in general terms, we can then apply the answer to the concrete case of academic achievement, and study the strategy of research dealing with failures to predict.

Why are the predictions from psychological and educational data less than perfect? Why are there errors in prediction?

Prediction falls short of perfection in the first place because of *errors of measurement*—errors of measurement both in the predictor and in what is being predicted. A single limited sample of an individual's behavior, observed during some limited period of time, is inevitably an undependable representation of the whole range of behavior that it is supposed to represent. A spelling test of 20 words, or 50 words, or even 100 words, given one day in school, will not correspond exactly with another test of a different 20, or 50, or 100 words given next week. Perfect accuracy is characteristic of neither the measure being used as a predictor nor the score or grade that it is supposed to predict. With both a fallible predictor and a fallible criterion, discrepancies between the two are inevitable, if for no other reason than the measurement errors in each. In research relating to achievement, we must be careful not to waste our time and effort in attempts to give explanations of discrepancies arising solely from these measurement errors. We must be especially careful not to design an experiment that allows these measurement errors to influence the results in some systematic way, and thus to distort the relationships that we are studying.

Prediction falls short of perfection in the second place because of the *heterogeneity of the criterion* that is to be predicted. If we are predicting occupational success, an income of $5,000 signifies one thing for a clergyman, something quite different for a banker. If we are predicting achievement, an "A" signifies one thing in physics, something else in vocational agriculture; one thing at Harvard, something else at Siwash State College. Different schools, different programs, even different instructors use the same symbol system with different meanings. The differences are partly of level, partly of kind. To the extent that these differences exist, we could not expect that those with a Scholastic Aptitude Test score of 500, for example, would uniformly get an average grade of "B," even if that score itself were perfectly reliable. It would depend upon which college, which program, which instructors.

The category of criterion heterogeneity merges into that of error of measurement in the criterion, and no entirely clear separation of the two is possible. Where no specific sources of heterogeneity of the sort just discussed can be isolated for study, criterion heterogeneity is functionally equivalent to measurement error. But often general sources of heterogeneity *can* be isolated and studied, and allowance can be made for them in the experimental design. The likelihood of encountering such heterogeneity, and the need to identify it, study it, and if possible eliminate it, define one aspect of our experimental problem.

A third reason why any set of predictions falls short of perfect accuracy is *limited scope in the predictors*. That is, the predictors that have been studied may include only part of the determiners of the criterion variable. All behavior is complexly determined. No one predictor will ever include *all* the determinants of a behavioral outcome. We have tended to become preoccupied with scholastic aptitude measures because they *do* correlate substantially with later achievement, and consequently do permit some improvement in the accuracy of predictions. But neither our psychological insights nor our statistical evidence give us reason to believe that a scholastic aptitude test measures *all* of the significant determiners of scholastic achievement. A legitimate and significant area of inquiry is the determination of other kinds of facts about an individual that can be shown to improve predictions. As we are able to extend our understanding of the relevant factors, increase the accuracy of our forecasts, and so reduce "overprediction," we will automatically reduce "underachievement."

The fourth and final category of reason for our failure to predict with precision is the *impact of varied experiences upon the individual* between the date the prediction is made and the date the criterion measure matures. When our prediction involves a genuine forecast over time—not a purely statistical "prediction" from concurrent measures—we must recognize the impact of events that occur during that time. Variations in quality and type of instruction, exposure to different kinds and amounts of remedial teaching, introduction of varied patterns of educational and personal guidance—all these interact with the characteristics of the person to determine what is learned. Furthermore, in any group of children there occur "chance" events which could hardly have been anticipated in advance—death of a parent, financial stringency, protracted illness—with varying effects upon the individual, depending upon his resources for coping with them. These produce a kind of irreducible minimum of departures of actual achievement from the most perfect and informed prediction.

Information about the quality of these temporally intervening variables is important, insofar as they can be described and known, if we are to improve the precision of our predictions of achievement. Manipulation of those aspects that are manipulable becomes important as a means of modifying achievement—not only for specific individuals but for the group as a whole. Recognition of them as "chance" or "contingency" factors helps further to understand why our predictions must remain forever imperfect.

We shall now need to examine these four sources of error in our predictions—(1) errors of measurement, (2) criterion heterogeneity, (3) limited scope in predictors, and (4) intervening experiences—somewhat more critically and in detail. After that we will review the main strategies for research dealing with the discrepancy between predicted and actual achievement—the so-called problem of "underachievement."

SOURCES OF DISCREPANCY BETWEEN PREDICTED AND ACTUAL ACHIEVEMENT

As we indicated in the previous section, students show discrepancies between measures of aptitude and of achievement for a number of reasons, and only a fraction of these represent modifiable features in the individual or in the educational situation in which he is placed. We must recognize certain statistical artifacts and methodological pit-falls and allow for their effects before we can begin to deal with what is educationally real and significant. A slightly different way of categorizing the discrepancies between pre-dicted and observed achievement, would point to four sources for these discrepancies. These are (1) errors of measurement in our tests or appraisals, (2) heterogeneity in the achievement, or criterion, variable, (3) essentially unmodifiable factors in the nature and background of the person, and only finally, (4) personal and edu-cational factors that are subject to manipulation or modification. Let us examine each of these in turn.

Errors of measurement

In part, we fail to find perfect correspondence between aptitude and achievement because of "errors of measurement" in our ap-praisals both of aptitude and of achievement. By "errors of measure-ment" we mean the combination of factors which make it impossi-ble to get *exactly* the same results from two experimentally independent measures of the same function. Thus, if we test a group of children with Form A of an aptitude test this week and with Form B next week, we will fail to get identical results for each individual, for a number of reasons. The most obvious reasons are:

1. The specific tasks in the two forms are different, and some children will be better able to do one set of tasks than the other.

2. Some children will feel better, work a little harder, or be a little more attentive on one occasion than on the other.

3. A certain amount of guessing at answers will take place, and some children will be more lucky on one occasion than the other.

There are probably other minor sources of inconsistency of per-formance that we do not readily identify, and to which we apply the inclusive label of "chance."

Since the error of measurement is conceived of as a random, chance variate associated only with a particular testing, it is also necessarily unrelated to any other measure, such as a measure of achievement. Just as there are discrepancies between two measures of the *same* function due to errors in each measurement, so also there must be discrepancies between two measures of *different* func-tions due to the errors of measurement in each. Thus some discrepancy is to be expected between *predicted* achievement based upon an aptitude measure and *actual* achievement based upon an achievement measure, merely because the aptitude and achievement measures both include within them errors of measurement.

How large discrepancies between predicted and obtained scores can we expect because of errors of measurement alone? By a little straightforward algebra, the following relationships can be demonstrated. (See Appendix A for derivation.)

Standard deviation of a
discrepancy score

$$S_D = S_C\sqrt{1 - r_{PC}^2} \tag{1}$$

Reliability of discrepancy
score

$$r_D = \frac{r_C + r_{PC}^2 r_P - 2r_{PC}^2}{1 - r_{PC}^2} \tag{2}$$

Standard deviation of
discrepancies arising
purely from errors of
measurement

$$S_{D\varepsilon} = S_C\sqrt{1 + r_{PC}^2 - r_C - r_P r_{PC}^2} \tag{3}$$

where S_D = standard deviation of discrepancy scores,

S_C = standard deviation of criterion scores,

$S_{D\varepsilon}$ = standard deviation of discrepancy scores due to error of measurement in predictor and criterion,

r_C = reliability of criterion measure,

r_P = reliability of predictor measure,

r_{PC} = correlation between predictor and criterion measure.

The standard deviation of a set of discrepancy scores gives a measure of the spread or scatter that may be expected in a set of differences between predicted and actual outcome or criterion measures, knowing the total spread of criterion scores in the group and the correlation between the criterion scores and a predictor. Thus, if we knew that the standard deviation of reading scores for 6th graders in a particular school was 1.00 grade-units and that the correlation between 6th grade reading and a 5th grade IQ test was .70, we would have

Standard deviation of discrepancy scores $= 1.00\sqrt{1 - (.70)^2} = .71$

In other words, the differences between the obtained reading grade-scores and those predicted from the earlier IQ would produce a frequency distribution with a standard deviation of about $7/10$ of a grade. If we assume a reasonable approximation to a normal curve, this would mean that we could occasionally expect to find pupils for whom there was a difference of as much as two full grades between actual and predicted reading level.

Now let us assume that the reliability of the predictor test is .90 and the reliability of the criterion measure is .80. (These values are fairly representative of the reliabilities that characterize tests that we are accustomed to use, as is the intercorrelation of .70 between an aptitude and a reading test.) Given these values, we find from formula (3) that

Standard deviation of discrepancies arising purely from errors of measurement
$$= 1.00\sqrt{1 + (.70)^2 - .80 - .90\,(.70)^2}$$
$$= 1.00\sqrt{1 + .49 - .80 - .44}$$
$$= 1.00\sqrt{0.25}$$
$$= 0.50$$

In other words, if *nothing* but the errors of measurement in the predictor and criterion were operating, we could *still* expect to get a spread of discrepancy scores represented by a standard deviation of half a grade-unit. We could *still* occasionally get discrepancies between predicted and actual reading level of as much as a grade and a half. This degree of "underachievement" would be possible as a result of nothing more than measurement error.

Formula (2) tells us that the reliability of the discrepancies between predicted and actual achievement, i.e., the reliability of the measure of degree of "underachievement," is given by

$$r_D = \frac{.80 + (.70)^2\,(.90) - 2\,(.70)^2}{1 - (.70)^2}$$

$$= \frac{.80 + .44 - .98}{1 - .49} = \frac{.26}{.51}$$

$$= .51$$

In terms of the reliabilities of the separate measures with which we started, i.e., .80 and .90, this discrepancy score is clearly a distressingly unstable measure. We must have relatively limited faith in the dependability of our diagnosis of any individual's "overachievement" or "underachievement." Thus, we must recognize that in the discrepancy between predicted and actual achievement we are usually dealing with a rather unreliable and fragile phenomenon, and one in which errors of measurement contribute a substantial fraction of the variation.

The often low reliability of discrepancy scores affects our experimental design in two ways. In the first place, the presence of a substantial component of error variance makes our experiments less sensitive. If "chance" contributes a large component to our data, any genuine underlying differences between groups or treatments are likely to be blurred and we will tend to get nonsignificant results. In correlational studies, correlations will tend to be small, and consequently not statistically significant unless we have large groups. Comparisons of extreme groups, really a type of correlational design (see pages 56 ff.), will less often show significant differences. With a less sensitive experimental design, it will be necessary to use larger numbers of cases in order to achieve the desired power in the final testing of our hypotheses. Thus, in contrast with the rather small groups that have often been used in studying "underachievement," large groups of subjects will be needed. A study based on a small number of individuals will be almost doomed to yield inconclusive results.

The second, and in many ways more serious, effect upon our research will come through possible systematic bias introduced into the results. The type of bias arises from what is known as the "regression effect." We must explore this effect at this point and examine its influence upon our experimental results.

Whenever the correlation between two measures is less than perfect, and especially when it is low, the individuals who fall well *above* average on one measure will be less superior on the other, and those who fall well *below* average on the first measure will be less inferior on the second. In the extreme case, when the correlation between the two measures is exactly zero, the persons who are at the top on measure X will tend to be neither above nor below average on measure Y, and this will be equally true of those who fall at the bottom on X. The situation will be represented by Diagram 1 in Figure 1. In this figure, each dot represents a person, and the swarm of dots shows how persons scatter out in the X and Y directions when the correlation between X and Y is approximately .00.

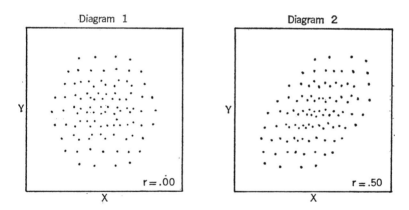

Figure I. Scatter-Plots for Correlations of .00 and .50

Diagram 1 in Figure 2 shows how things would look if we took a slice of high-scorers on X and a group of low-scorers on X, and looked at their distribution of Y-scores. Each slice has the same mean, and the mean for each slice corresponds to that for the total group. Diagram 2 in Figures 1 and 2 shows the situation for a moderate correlation of about .50. The Y-score distributions of the two slices (based on X-score) now have different means, but the two means differ much less than (actually, about .50 times as much as) do the X-scores for the two slices.

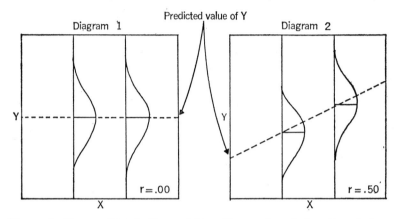

Figure 2. Y-score Distributions at Two X-score Levels for Correlations of .00 and .50

This relationship is described, in basic statistics, in terms of the *regression equation* for predicting Y from X. The predicted Y-score, which is a mathematical estimate of the average Y-score for the slice corresponding to a given X-score, is given as

$$\tilde{z}_y = r_{xy} z_x$$

where $\tilde{z}_y$ is the predicted Y-score, expressed in standard-score units,
   z_x is the known X-score, also expressed in standard-score units, and
   r_{xy} is the correlation between X and Y.

Thus, from this formula, a group deviating from the mean score on X by an amount equal to z_x will, on the average, deviate from the mean Y-score by an amount that is r_{xy} times as great. So, if $r_{xy} = .50$, we may expect a group *picked because of its X-score* to be only .50 times as outstanding on Y. (The relationship holds in reverse, also. If we had picked the group because it was outstanding on Y, it would turn out to be only half as outstanding on X.)

Thus, if a group is selected on the basis of high score on some administration of an aptitude test, the members will in general do less well on an achievement measure. They will "regress" down toward the average value in the group. By the same token, those below average on the aptitude measure will show a regression upward on the achievement measure. If a simple difference between aptitude and achievement standard scores, or a ratio of achievement to aptitude measure, is computed, the high aptitude group will appear primarily to be "underachievers" and the low aptitude group to be "overachievers." For this reason it is necessary to define "underachievement" as discrepancy of actual achievement from the *predicted* value, predicted upon the basis of the regression equation between aptitude and achievement. A failure to recognize this regression effect has rendered questionable, if not meaningless, much of the research on "underachievement." A few examples will serve to illustrate some of the common errors.

Diener [1],* working with college students, picked out two groups who showed the largest discrepancies between the American Council on Education Psychological Examination and college grade point average. Those with higher percentiles on the ACE than on GPA were designated "underachievers," of course, and those with higher percentiles on GPA than on ACE were called "overachievers." But when the scores of the two groups are examined, it is found that they differ as much on the aptitude test as on the achievement measure. This can be seen in the following table.

| | "Overachieving" Students | | "Underachieving" Students | | |
	Mean	*S.D.*	*Mean*	*S.D.*	*t*
ACE	76.53	26.22	131.64	17.32	14.74
GPA	3.84	0.79	1.93	0.87	11.94

Thus, the "underachievers" could just as truly be called "overintelligent," and the "overachievers" called "underintelligent." The method of selection resulted in groups that were different, and about equally different, on both measures. Consider only the "un-

* Numbers in brackets refer to the numbered References on page 79.

derachiever" group for a moment. Since the way of picking students for this group picked ones who were above average on ACE, we can feel assured that they would regress back to a somewhat lower average aptitude score if a second measure of aptitude were obtained, because the correlation between the two measures would be less than perfect. Again, if we were able to get a second appraisal of their achievement, it would regress upward. Thus, the discrepancy between aptitude and achievement in this group is certainly overestimated as a result of the way in which the group was selected, and would diminish if they were retested.

A different pattern is illustrated in a study by Kingston and George [5] comparing reading gains in college students who had and had not taken a remedial reading course. The initial comprehension scores of the remedial readers had been about one full standard deviation lower than those of the comparison group. If one could assume that the cases were selected for the remedial group in part on the basis of low initial reading test score, which seems a reasonable assumption, then one could predict that there would be some gain on a second testing, due simply to regression toward the mean, even if one had no more than passed his hand over the students' heads before he retested them; and part, at least, of the gain of the remedial group can be attributed to simple regression upwards toward the mean. A second problem in this study is that those who dropped out of college before junior year did not get included in the final analyses. Thus further bias was probably introduced, in that those who were *truly* the worst readers, and whose reading would have tended to show up less well on the second testing, tended to be eliminated from the study.

As a final illustration, let us consider a study by Mouly and Grant [7]. In this study, a group of children had been identified whose reading age was at least a year behind their mental age, the average difference being 17 months. The pupils were given special treatment in reading centers for an unspecified period, and then retested with the reading test. No control group was used, so it was impossible to allow for simple practice effects on the reading test, or for regression effects resulting from the way the group was chosen.

One analysis that was made, however, was a study of the relationship of amount of gain per month to amount of initial retardation. As we would predict purely from our knowledge of the regression effect, the more retarded gained more. That is, the larger the difference between achievement and aptitude the more the achievement measure tended to regress upward toward average upon a second testing.

In summary, a first source of discrepancy between predicted and actual achievement is *error of measurement* in both the predictor measures and the achievement criterion that is being predicted. As errors of measurement become large, especially when the correlation between predictor and predicted is high, the discrepancies that occur may arise primarily from errors of measurement, and individual differences in size of the discrepancy may be attributable largely to chance. This will tend to reduce substantially the sensitivity of any studies of the correlates of such discrepancies. Errors of measurement become especially troublesome when groups are selected for study in some way that systematically capitalizes upon the measurement errors.

Heterogeneity in the achievement or criterion variable

Any investigation of achievement relative to expectation depends upon some measure of the achievement variable. This measure serves as the criterion of what each individual has actually achieved. It is discrepancies between this *actual* achievement and the *predicted* achievement, predicted from some measure or measures of aptitude, that are designated "over-" or "underachievement." The criterion measure of achievement may sometimes be score on a standardized test; more often it is a composite of teachers' marks. Whatever the criterion measure we use, it is crucial that it be substantially the same measure for all the cases in our group. Otherwise we will get discrepancies between predicted achievement and actual achievement because our achievement measure itself changes, and signifies different things for different individuals.

Of course, we must expect that there will be errors of measurement in a criterion measure of achievement, just as there are in any predictor test of aptitude. The basic unreliability of an achievement test or of a teacher's marking procedures is one half of the picture that we were discussing in the previous section. Insofar as these errors of measurement in the criterion are random, unsystematic, and unpredictable, they produce random and unpredictable discrepancies between predictor and criterion variables.

The criterion heterogeneity that we are now talking about, however, is the heterogeneity that is associated in a *systematic* way with known or knowable external facts about the criterion. Criterion heterogeneity would arise in its most blatant form if we were to mix the records of 10 students from Harvard with those of 100 from Podunk State Teachers College, and study the relationship between a scholastic aptitude test and college grade point average. If we used the single common regression equation based on Podunk students, we could predict that practically all of the Harvard students would be "underachievers"—i.e., they would get lower grades than predicted from the regression of Podunk grades on the aptitude test. With aptitude ratings that would lead one to predict "A" averages at Podunk, our Harvard students would be getting only "C"s. The difference would be due *not* to the fact that Harvard provides in some way an extremely unstimulating environment for learning. It would be due to the extreme heterogeneity of our criterion, a heterogeneity so great that on an absolute scale of achievement a "C" at Harvard signifies a higher level of achievement than an "A" at Podunk. We would have been combining, and treating as if they were the same, score scales on our criterion that had completely different significance.

One does not find in actual studies heterogeneity as extreme as would be true in the example that we have just described. However, the problem is a very real one. Thus, in Diener's study [1] referred to earlier, in which discrepancy between scholastic aptitude test and grade point average was the basis for defining "over-" and "underachievement," more of the "overachievers" were enrolled in agriculture or education. More of the "underachievers" were in liberal arts or engineering. Thus, what this particular study demonstrated, in part, was that academic standards are higher and the intellectual demands more severe in a school of engineering than in a school of agriculture or education. Hardly a profound finding! In the meantime, any other factors that distinguished between engineering and agriculture students would tend to be related to "underachievement." In this research the investigator was studying a difference that was in part meaningless, a difference that stemmed from the criterion rather than from characteristics of the students.

Whenever we combine data from different schools, different programs, or even different teachers, we are likely to introduce heterogeneity into the criterion. If it is possible to identify discrete groups of this sort, one can test to see whether a single regression of criterion on predictor applies to all the subgroups. Analysis of covariance is the appropriate statistical technique for this purpose.* It tells us whether all subgroups can be considered to share a common regression line—common with respect both to slope and to constant term. Whenever the analysis shows that a single common regression does *not* apply to some one of the groups, then it is necessary to determine predicted achievement from the specific regression line for that group. Thus, we might have a regression line for predicting engineering school grades quite different from the regression line applicable to the school of agriculture, or one for predicting grades in an honors section of a subject different from the one that would apply to the regular section.

In summary, then, in any research on "over-" or "underachievement," we must beware lest our criterion measure of achievement itself be heterogeneous, the same score or symbol representing different real levels of performance in different subgroups. If there are different identifiable subgroups among our experimental subjects, for which different standards of performance may perhaps hold, we should use analysis of covariance to see whether a common regression of criterion on predictor holds throughout the groups. If it does not, then we dare not combine the groups in a common study. We must establish predicted achievement separately within

---

* Analysis of covariance is treated in standard statistics texts. For example, see Walker and Lev [9].

each subgroup, and base our measure of discrepancy on a predicted achievement determined in this way.

Stable relatively unmodifiable factors

An individual's standing on a measure of achievement depends in part upon stable, relatively unmodifiable factors in the individual's nature or his background. Within limits, an aptitude measure is one such factor. We use the aptitude measure as a predictor of achievement because we believe that it tells us something pretty fundamental and lasting about the person. But the aptitude score is only one fact that characterizes a person. There are many others, and a number of these may also have some significance as predictors of his achievement.

Thus, we find that achievement as measured by teachers' grades depends upon whether the pupil is a boy or girl. Most of the "underachievers" in a mixed group are boys; more of the "achievers" are girls. Through some combination of industry, docility, and agreeableness girls manage to make a more favorable impression on their teachers than boys do—a differential that is not generally maintained on coldly impersonal standardized achievement tests. If we are to study *other* factors relating to achievement, we are well advised to work within a group of the same sex, and to base our regression equation for predicting achievement upon a group all of the same sex. Otherwise anything that characterizes boys more than it does girls will tend to be associated with "underachievement." A number of investigators have recognized this, and have planned their experiments to take care of it, either by limiting their study to pupils of only one sex or by analyzing the results for each sex separately.

Sex is only one of many stable, unchangeable factors that may be related to the aptitude–achievement discrepancy. Factors of family background, such as parental education or family socioeconomic status represent another. Thus, Frankel [2] found that "achievers" at Bronx High School of Science came from better home backgrounds with higher socioeconomic status and better educated fathers than did "underachievers."

It should be pointed out that factors such as sex, race, or socio-economic status are not in any *direct* sense *causes* of high or low achievement. Categories such as these serve as ready labels by which we identify subgroups of people for whom the total environmental context is different. Thus, both our schools and our society set subtly different social and intellectual environments for girls and for boys. Boys are expected to be independent, somewhat aggressive, interested in things mechanical and scientific; girls are expected (even today, we suspect) to be "sweet," docile, somewhat domestic, and interested in things verbal and artistic. The middle-class social background emphasizes striving and achievement, and the importance of academic success, in a way that the lower-class environment does not. And certainly the expectations of society and the values of the group itself differ in many subtle ways for the Caucasian and the Negro. All of these differences are phenomena worthy of study in their own right, in order to understand the nature of the differences and the ways in which they interact with the school environment. But for us now, the important thing is that these stable characteristics of the individual or his environment do function as determiners of his school achievement.

Sex and socioeconomic status are not things that the school is going to modify. Like aptitude, they are predictors of certain indicators of achievement. The investigator concerned with "underachievement" must be concerned with these factors, but his concern is to identify them and use them as additional variables in his prediction equation, not to manipulate them experimentally or use them in some practical way. Thus, a fully adequate prediction equation for indicating expected achievement will involve many variates. It will be an equation involving one or several measures of aptitude, sex, family background, and any other variates that have been found to improve the accuracy of forecasting school performance. "Underachievement" will then be understood as achievement falling below what would be forecast from our most informed and accurate prediction, based on a team of predictor variables.

In summary, then, stable and relatively unmodifiable factors of the sort we are considering in this section are important for a research program on "underachievement." It is important that we study them so that we may determine which ones of them function as additional predictors of achievement. We can then use them to improve our prediction so that it will be more informed and accurate. "Over-" and "underachievement" will then be defined as discrepancies of actual achievement from predicted achievement, when the predictions are made in this more refined way. As our predictions become more accurate, the discrepancies will become smaller, and the spread between the total discrepancy variance and the discrepancy variance due to errors of measurement will become less. It is only this residue that falls in our fourth category, discussed below.

Personal and educational factors subject to manipulation and modification

Modifiability and manipulability exist in varying degrees. Some aspects of the educational and social environment to which a child is exposed can be changed very readily. Thus, he can be moved to a different seat, given reading material of a different level of difficulty, given access to a "teaching machine," or given special teaching by a remedial teacher. Other aspects can be changed only with great difficulty. In this category might come a mother's tendency to overprotect a child, or the tendency of the close friends of the pupil to regard school achievement as "sissy." The modifiable shades off by imperceptible degrees into the unmodifiable. But there is a domain within which the school or society can make changes, hoping that these changes will result in better achievement on the part of the pupil.

These areas of possible modification represent the main focus of research concern in work on "over-" and "underachievement." They are the areas of possible constructive pay-off. We wish to identify relationships within this domain, and we wish to move in and modify that which can be modified, to see if deficiencies in achievement can be overcome.

Within this domain our research approach may be either correlational or experimental. Thus, we may get our initial understanding of the ways in which certain modifiable factors influence achieve-ment by seeing how they are *related* to achievement in different pupils. But correlational studies are less satisfying than experimental studies in which a particular element in the situation is actually modified and the results of the modification are observed. This is true whether the interest be scientific or practical. From the point of view of scientific understanding, the "if–then" relationship is much more clearly established if after one factor is experimentally modified a change is observed, than when one merely observes a going-togetherness. From the practical point of view, when actual modification of the educational or social environment in some way is followed by gains in achievement, we feel that we have provided a demonstration both of what to do and of how to do it. So we may either engage in correlational studies relating achievement to mod-ifiable variables or in experimental studies in which certain vari-ables are in fact modified, but so far as our ingenuity permits we should try to cast studies of these factors into the experimental pattern. Studies of the influence of special reading instruction on achievement illustrate the research pattern of experimentally manip-ulating educational variables and then evaluating changes in an achievement criterion variable. At the same time, the better designed of these show the types of precautions in experimental design that must be observed if one is to get meaningful results.

McDonald [6], for example, studied the effect of participation in a special reading program upon college grades during subsequent semesters. Those who had received remedial instruction were com-pared with a control group of individuals who had also applied for the course but who could not be accommodated. No statement is made of the basis for deciding who was to be admitted from among the group of applicants; the possibility of some selective factor in admissions still exists, and weakens the design of the study. However, one point that the author believes to make for equiva-lence in motivation is that the control group members were suffi-ciently interested to come around and take the same battery of tests that was used with the remedial reading groups.

Tests of aptitude and initial level of reading achievement were obtained for members of both the experimental and control groups. An analysis of covariance based upon these variables was used to control for any differences between the groups in the background variables. This type of analysis makes the results become in effect a study of that part of college grades *not* accounted for by the background variables of initial aptitude and reading ability. Under these circumstances, the investigators found significantly better grades for the remedial reading group than for the control group during the following semester, and fewer drop-outs from college in the remedial group.

A somewhat different type of study was that of Stamatakos and Shaffer [8], in which four groups of intellectually superior freshmen were formed on the basis of random assignment in advance of any experimental treatment. Assignment at random to the different experimental treatments rules out all but chance differences between the treatment groups. The possibility of any systematic bias favoring one group over the others is eliminated. This aspect of design is very important for clear and interpretable results. The four groups were given different amounts and types of special attention aimed at stimulating their academic achievement. The differences between groups were not statistically significant, so there was no evidence that any of the procedures were effective. Thus, the experiment is of interest for its relatively clear design rather than for its findings.

Summary statement

Reviewing research strategy in relation to the four sources of aptitude–achievement discrepancy that we have discussed above, we may conclude as follows:

1. We must recognize the presence of errors of measurement and arrange our investigation in such a way that we do not capitalize upon these errors to produce spurious effects.

2. We must carry out our investigation within a population for which a given score on the criterion variable has uniform meaning, or so adjust the obtained criterion scores that they *do* have uniform meaning.

3. We must study the stable background factors that can lead to a more accurate prediction of achievement, and incorporate them into our prediction so that it becomes maximally accurate.

4. We must study, and if possible manipulate, the plausible modifiable variables in order to learn to what extent education can overcome whatever real discrepancies between actual and predicted achievement still remain.

THE MAIN DESIGNS
FOR RESEARCH ON "UNDERACHIEVEMENT"

As in most fields of educational and psychological research, investigations into the discrepancies between predicted and actual achievement may proceed either by experimental manipulation of variables or by an examination of the relationships that are found among variables. As applied to the area of "underachievement," the first approach implies identification of a group of "underachievers" and then systematic modification of some aspect of the educational environment for part of the group. The experimental populations must then be followed up at a later point in time, and a comparison made of the achievements of those who have received and those who have not received the special educational treatment. In other words, an "experiment," in the classical sense, is carried out.

The second approach is one of studying relationships, as they are found in the natural setting. We examine directly the possibilities of prediction in the statistical sense, and only indirectly the possibilities of modification and control of learning. The prediction may be a genuine prediction over time, as when aptitude test scores, previous school record, and perhaps other factors known in advance of entry into a particular school program are correlated with subsequent success in that program. Or the prediction may be only a statistical prediction from one to another of concurrently obtained variables, as when a measure of some aspect of motivation is correlated with a score on an achievement test. There are enough real differences between these two designs, and between the issues that arise as we try to apply them, to make it desirable to consider each separately.

The study of relationships among pairs or sets of variables is carried out most clearly and explicitly by studying intact groups. The nature of relationships can then be studied throughout the full range of each variable, and the results expressed in terms of correlation, linear regression, or (if it seems desirable) some more complex functional relationship. However, there is a certain appeal to basing one's research on sharply contrasting groups, and many investigators have succumbed to this appeal. In this pattern, extreme groups are selected from the total population. When the area of investigation is "underachievement," the groups are usually the "overachieving" and "underachieving" tails of a distribution of relative achievement. These two groups are then studied to see in what other ways they differ—i.e., to identify correlates of "over-" and "underachievement." The comparison of extreme groups is basically an implicit and incomplete correlational method, in which the intermediate cases have been dropped out.

In the following pages, we shall examine some of the special problems that arise as each of the above four variations of method is applied to the investigation of "underachievement." In recapitulation, the research designs can be classified as follows:

    I. Experimental manipulation of variables.

    II. Correlational studies of relationships.

        A. Actual forecasting over a period of time.

        B. Concurrent correlation among variables.

        C. Study of contrasting groups.

A section will be devoted to each of these approaches.

2

Design I: Experimental Manipulation
and Follow-up

The first design that we have identified for studying "underachievement" conforms to the classical pattern of experimental research
in psychology or education. Two or more groups are set up that are
initially equivalent. They are then exposed to different experimental treatments, final level of achievement is measured, and the
achievements of the different treatment groups are compared. The
only way in which the design is distinctive is that ordinarily the
experimental groups are composed of students who have done poorly
in school work or in some measure of school achievement, and one
or more of the treatments is likely to be a "remedial" treatment
designed to overcome the deficiency.

Overt manipulation of experimental variables is always a satisfying approach to understanding, and even to controlling, educational
and psychological outcomes; so this pattern for investigation is a
very appropriate one. The educator's practical concern with de-
ficient educational achievement is to remedy the condition. If we
can identify significant variables in the learning experience of students, perhaps especially of students who have been encountering
difficulty, and can manipulate these variables in such a way that
the difficulties are overcome, the results may have both theoretical
importance for our understanding of the learning process and practical importance for our "engineering" of the educational enterprise.

Though the general problems in this pattern are much the same as those in all investigations involving the manipulation of experimental variables, they have certain specifics in the context of "underachievement" studies which merit our closer scrutiny.

CRUCIAL ROLE OF AN ADEQUATE CONTROL GROUP

In research on improving the learning of "underachievers," as in any educational research designed to test the effect of an experimental treatment, data for an adequate control group are of critical importance. The mere fact of gain is, of course, inadequate to demonstrate the effectiveness of the experimental treatment. Firstly, there is the possibility of a simple practice effect, so that merely having taken a test may enable one to do somewhat better on it a second time. To show that an experimental procedure is a desirable procedure, it is necessary to compare its effectiveness with some "standard," or usual, procedure and determine whether it is in fact better. However, an additional and more subtle effect operates when we are dealing with "underachievers," as "underachievement" is typically defined, that makes a control group even more essential and helps to define the nature of an adequate control group. This effect is a statistical artifact of regression arising out of the fact that we (1) have appreciable errors of measurement (see pages 7–15) and (2) may have selected our sample of experimental cases in such a way that these errors of measurement systematically bias the results. Let us examine this point a little more fully.

Whenever we identify a group of "underachievers," we are dealing with a group of pupils who have done less well on some measure of achievement than we would have predicted on the basis of an aptitude test or some other fact that we know about them. Picking a group so as to maximize the discrepancies between achievement and aptitude does in part identify a group of genuinely poor achievers, but it also capitalizes on those who have been *under-measured* by that particular achievement testing—i.e., those who were inattentive, indisposed, or unlucky so far as *that specific testing* was concerned, so that they had predominantly negative "errors of measurement." By definition "errors of measurement" are uncorrelated from one testing to another, so the "errors of measurement" for this group will, on the average, be approximately zero on a subsequent testing. The upshot is that a group so selected will tend to do better collectively on a subsequent testing, even if we only wave a magic wand over them between the two testings.

In view of the above it is essential not only that a control group be used, but also that the control group be comparable to the group receiving the experimental treatment with respect to degree of "underachievement." It is not sufficient that the gains in achievement test score of the experimental group over some period of instruction be compared with the published test norms, or with the gains of some classes of normal achievers receiving standard instruction. The control group should also consist of "underachievers" comparable in ability and in achievement to the experimental group. This precaution is important in order that any regression effects may operate with equal force in both groups.

Of course, there are other respects in which it is important that the control group be comparable to the experimental group. Some are relatively tangible factors such as sex and socioeconomic status. But at least as important are a group of intangibles to which, for lack of a better collective label, we will apply the designation "motivation." Whenever being chosen to receive some special experimental treatment depends upon the initiative of the individual in applying or volunteering for the treatment, or whenever it depends upon a judgment by a teacher that the student is likely to respond to or profit from the treatment, the experimental sample is likely to be a biased one. This possibility is always present when the experimental group is a naturally occurring one, made up of those who did in fact receive a certain treatment, and the control group is a synthetic one, made up *after the fact* to match the experimental group on one or more externally visible factors such as age, sex, socioeconomic status or aptitude test score. Under these circumstances, the control group is likely to include those who were not interested enough to apply for special help, or those whom the responsible school officer didn't consider likely to profit from the special help. If they do in fact perform less well than the experimental group, it may be due to their nature rather than to the fact that they failed to receive the experimental treatment.

The ideal design for an experiment involving contrasting treatments is one in which pairs * of pupils are made up in advance, the members of a given pair being as much alike as possible on one or more variables that are likely to be related to the final criterion measure, and in which the assignment of one member of the pair to the experimental group and the other to the control group is then made entirely at random. This is the only way that we can be *sure* that there are no subtle systematic biases differentiating one group from the other and that only chance differences remain to cloud the effect of the experimental variable.

Really random assignment to treatments has been extremely rare in educational investigations concerned with overcoming deficiencies in achievement. Educational concern has typically been practical and humanitarian. Educators have been loath to deny a treatment to a student they thought might be helped by it. They have been concerned primarily with using their techniques, and only secondarily with evaluating them. The net result has been that almost all evaluations have been fallible in the sense that the control and experimental groups were not *really* drawn at random from the same population, and the experimenter has never been able to be sure that they were equivalent. Some investigators have been quite conscious of this problem [6, 8] and have used various devices to try to minimize it—e.g., using as a control group those who applied for service but had to be refused because the quota for the special class was already full. Any such procedures which reduce differences between experimental and control groups are all to the good. However, they are at best an expedient for approximating the goal of random assignment to treatments.

Let us reaffirm that in those cases in which random assignment to control and experimental groups is possible, an empirical comparison of different treatments gives one of the best ways of getting understanding and control of achievement deficiencies. The typical

---

* Sets of three or more if there are three or more treatments.

procedure of synthesizing a control group after the fact is far inferior in terms of the sureness and conviction with which it provides knowledge. One cannot express this degree of inferiority in any quantitative terms. It varies from case to case, depending upon the probability that biasing factors have been at work, and the degree to which it has been possible to pick the control group in such a way that these factors have been minimized.

LOSS OF SUBJECTS

A further problem, somewhat related to that of obtaining a completely adequate control group, is loss of cases from the experimental group. When individuals undertake some special program of remedial instruction, especially if they enter upon it of their own choice and initiative, some are likely to drop out of the program or be dropped from it before it is completed. There is very good chance that those who do not complete the program are those who are less well-motivated or those who for some other reason are not profiting from the program. If this is the case, then those who complete the program are a biased sample of those who started it. They will tend to show a favorable performance because the ones who performed unfavorably dropped out of the group along the way.

In terms of experimental design, this means that when a comparison is being made between an experimental treatment and a control treatment, it is important to get criterion data on *all* members of both groups, whether they complete the special treatment or not. It may be desirable to make a separate analysis of the cases that drop out of the experiment, but some analysis of them should be undertaken whenever possible. In particular, such a separate analysis can be expected to throw some light on whether there was a tendency to retain in the experimental group only those who are making satisfactory progress. By contrast, if analyses are made *only* of those who have completed the training and if there have been an appreciable number who have failed to complete it, one can never be really sure whether the results for those who have remained are to be attributed to the *effect* of the experimental treatment or the *selectivity* of the treatment.

The more general problem of dropping out of school also serves to complicate comparison of an experimental and a control treatment. However, this kind of drop-out is quite different in its meaning and impact. It may affect experimental and control group alike. It actually serves as one criterion measure of the success of an experimental treatment. If the academic survival rate is higher in an experimental than in a control sample, this is one indication that the experimental treatment is proving helpful. However, one must then recognize that the meaning of any comparison of those who remain in the sample has been obscured. If varying percents of attrition due to academic failure have taken place in the experimental and control samples, the mean achievement of those who are left is in differing degrees biased by that attrition. Comparisons may still be suggestive, but they cannot be definitive, and the application of rigorous significance tests to score differences for the remaining cases is not really justified.

When there have been drop-outs for academic failure, it may at times be reasonable to assign some criterion score to the drop-outs and include them in statistical analyses. Thus, if the criterion of achievement were college freshman grade point average, it might seem reasonable to use the grade point average at the time of drop-out, if one could be determined, to represent grade point average for the year. However, any such procedure is somewhat arbitrary, and results must be interpreted with a degree of tentativeness.

MEANINGFULNESS OF EXPERIMENTAL VARIABLES

One problem in all educational research is that of describing the experimental treatment sufficiently exactly so that someone else can reproduce it. Thus, merely to say that the experimental group received "twenty hours of remedial instruction in reading" gives only the vaguest notion of what actually went on. Educational conditions and treatments are inevitably complex, involving a host of dimensions and of specific events. The choice of the aspects that are of central significance in describing what took place calls for the highest level of wisdom on the part of the investigator. We do not have an explicit and satisfactory taxonomy of educational in-put variables. All we can do is re-emphasize the importance of (1) selecting genuinely significant factors to vary in different experimental treatments and (2) describing in precise terms the essential components of that which has been varied.

CONTAMINATION OF CRITERION VARIABLES

It is perhaps worth while to call attention in passing to two or three possible sources of contamination of the criterion scores which may make fair evaluation of the effects of an experimental treatment difficult, if not impossible. First, we can call attention to the "Hawthorne effect," so named from a series of well-known experiments in which it was dramatically demonstrated. This is the effect that stems merely from being part of an experiment. The suggestion is that it is less important *what* one does to an experimental group than that one is doing *something*. Just being in an experiment, receiving special attention, and being at the center of the stage appears to influence performance, presumably through increasing motivation and effort. The effect may be expected to be temporary, and to evaporate as the excitement of being part of an experiment wears off. However, most evaluations of educational experiments are carried out over a limited time period, so that this effect is one to be reckoned with. In all educational research, we face the problem of judging how much to discount this influence. The problem applies in the same way to evaluation of remedial procedures applied to those who are not doing too well educationally. We must try to differentiate between the general motivational impact of receiving *some* type of special treatment and the specific value of the treatment that is given. Of course, one way to do this is to contrast two or more treatments, each of which is given the flavor of an experiment.

A second source of contamination may arise if the special treatment is related too specifically to the criterion measures. We refer here to more or less direct "coaching" for the criterion test. The line between practicing relevant skills and coaching for the final test is sometimes a fine one. If evaluation instruments sample sufficiently broadly from the domain involved and if instructors have no advance contact with the specific criterion tests, this problem is not likely to be serious.

A third possibility of contamination arises when the criterion measure involves subjective judgments by the teacher, experimenter, or others. If an essay test is to be graded, some product is to be judged, or ratings are to be made of aspects of individual performance or personality, awareness that a particular subject has been in one or another of the treatment groups may influence the judgment. The possibility of unconscious biases in judgment always exists when subjective judgments are being used. Steps should be taken to control the possibility. When it is an examination or other product to be evaluated, the surest procedure is to keep the rater in ignorance of the identity of the author of the paper or product being evaluated. The ideal procedure, whether the comparison is of different treatment groups or of performance before and after the treatment, is to have all products mixed together, so that they cannot be identified with a particular group or time of testing, and to have all of them appraised at the same time by the same group of judges.

SUMMARY STATEMENT

Comparison of the effect of different treatments applied to pupils whose performance falls below that which is expected or acceptable is one sound way of investigating the problem of remedying "underachievement." The most crucial step in designing such a study is that of obtaining a really adequate control group, so that one can determine what part of any observed gains are to be attributed to the experimental treatment. Randomized assignment of matched cases to treatment groups is to be preferred. Some type of criterion score should be sought for every case in both experimental and control group. Precautions should be taken to assure that the criterion score is not allowed to be contaminated by the group to which the individual belongs.

3

Design II-A: Prediction Over Time

Much of the research relating to "over-" and "underachievement" has been cast in the form of studies of the relationships with achievement arising in the natural school and life environment. One approach to studying the determiners of achievement, and in fact of defining expected achievement, is to find what variables correlate with achievement, how much they correlate with achievement, and how they are related to each other.

If we wish to determine what facts and factors can be used to predict how much an individual will learn and what he will achieve in school, the straightforward way to do so is to obtain for each person being studied one or more predictor measures and then to follow up and find out how much each person achieves. We can then study the relationships of the predictor measures, taken singly and in combination, to the criterion of achievement. When the research is on "underachievement," one or more of the predictors are used to define the expected achievement for each student. The other variables are studied with the hope that they may help to explain the discrepancies between "expected achievement," thus defined, and actual achievement. However, this division of predictor variables into two categories is an arbitrary and artificial one. What we are basically interested in is increasing our understanding of the conditions making for educational success or failure, and increasing the accuracy with which we are able to predict what the pupil will achieve. If it were not for practical matters having to do with (1) the lapse of time between the initial testing and the final maturing of criterion measures of achievement and (2) the cost of measuring groups large enough to yield stable results, this would almost always be the preferred method of studying factors related to educational outcomes.

The basic design of prediction over time gets us involved in the smallest number of questionable assumptions of any correlational method, and is widely useful. Let us specify conditions to be met if this design is to be used fruitfully, and offer some guides as to appropriate patterns and controls.

SELECTION OF PREDICTOR VARIABLES

In any correlational study of predictors of achievement, one's objective is to identify new and additional variables that will add to and improve the accuracy of prediction. Therefore, the set of predictor variables studied should include not only promising new predictors but also measures of the main categories of variables that have already been established as significantly correlated with final level of achievement. The most obvious of these categories are (1) initial level of achievement and (2) scholastic aptitude or general intelligence.

For any subject in which instruction has already been given prior to the start of the period covered by an investigation, final achievement will almost certainly be substantially related to initial achievement at the beginning of the experimental period. If our interest is in the learning that has taken place during the experimental period, i.e., in the gain in achievement, it is imperative that we measure initial status, so that this factor can be taken into account in any evaluation of other predictors of final achievement. Unless some other predictor adds to the prediction of final achievement that is possible from initial status alone, that variable is useless as a predictor of *learning*. Inital status may be represented sometimes by score on a standardized test and sometimes by previous course grades.

The second type of predictor that should usually be included, because it is so accepted as a predictor of academic achievement, is the conventional type of scholastic aptitude or "IQ" test. In some cases, a test of this type will add relatively little predictive effectiveness to what is already provided by a measure of initial status in the achievement area itself—for example, to an initial reading measure, if we are trying to predict final level of achievement in reading. However, the roles of initial achievement and of scholastic aptitude as predictors of final achievement are so well established that the investigator would practically always want to know how much any additional factor or factors *added* to the prediction possible from one of these two or, preferably, from both of them in combination.

In specific achievement areas, prior research may suggest certain other factors that have consistently shown a relationship to gains in achievement. It will pay to include measures of as many of these as possible in any study directed primarily at studying additional new factors, so that the relationship of the new factors to those already studied may be determined, and so that the unique contribution of the new factors may be established.

In general, then, in a correlational study that undertakes to identify predictors of final achievement, one should include measures of (1) initial achievement, (2) scholastic aptitude, (3) other effective predictors identified from previous research, and (4) the new predictor variables which are the focus of interest in the study.

INCLUSION OF AN ADEQUATE SAMPLE

If research is to be worth reporting, it must be based on a sample of cases of adequate size. The realistic investigator knows that the bulk of the prediction of final achievement level will be contributed by initial achievement and/or level of scholastic aptitude. When he studies the supplementary contribution of other variables, he studies a rather fragile and unstable phenomenon. To get a measure of the increment in prediction resulting from additional predictors that will be sufficiently stable and precise to be meaningful it will be necessary that he use samples of very substantial size. We can illustrate this point by an hypothetical example.

	1	2	3	4
1: Initial level of achievement	—	.50	.40	.70
2: Scholastic aptitude	.50	—	.35	.50
3: Experimental test	.40	.35	—	.45
4: Final level of achievement	.70	.50	.45	—

Consider the table of correlations given above. Variable *4*, final level of achievement, is the variable that we are trying to predict. All three of the other variables correlate quite substantially with final achievement. For a sample of any size greater than 35, a statistician would report that all of the correlations with variable *4*, were significantly different from zero (at the .01 level). Thus, if we had done our experiment with a sample of 40 cases, we could assert that our experimental test, variable *3*, showed a significant correlation with final level of achievement.

But suppose we now ask the question: Does our experimental test have a significant correlation with *gain* in achievement? We cannot answer this question with only the information given in the above correlation table. However, if we also know the relative sizes of the standard deviations of the initial and final achievement scores, then the standard formula for the correlation of differences * can give us the correlation of any predictor variable with gain from initial to final test. The table below shows the correlation with gain in achievement under three different assumptions as to the amount by which variability in achievement has increased at the end of the training period.

Final S.D. ÷ initial S.D.	Correlation with gain in achievement	Required sample size
1.5	.256	105
1.3	.198	173
1.1	.116	496

---

* This formula takes the form

$$r_{(y-x)z} = \frac{S_y r_{yz} - S_x r_{xz}}{\sqrt{S_y^2 + S_x^2 - 2S_y S_x r_{xy}}}$$

where x is initial achievement,
$\quad\;\; y$ is final achievement, and
$\quad\;\; z$ is the experimental test.

In each case, the correlation of the experimental test with individual differences in *gain* is less than the correlation with individual differences in *level* of final achievement. The correlation with gain is least when the increase in variance is least, and this is reasonable because it means in effect that individual differences in initial score constitute a larger part of individual differences in final score. The implication of the smaller correlation with gain is that a much larger sample of cases will be required if we are to be able to conclude that our observed correlation is significantly different from zero. In the illustration, the required numbers are about 105, 170, and 500, in the three cases, or roughly 3, 5, and 12 times as many as are required for the correlation of .45 with final status given in the table.

Another way to look at this same question would be to ask what weights we should apply to initial status, scholastic aptitude, and our experimental test if they were to be used in a regression equation * to give the best prediction of final status. The weights that give the best prediction are .548, .165, and .173 respectively for initial status, scholastic aptitude, and the experimental test. From the formula for the standard error of a regression weight,** we can calculate how large the sample would have to be in order for the weight of .173 to be significant at the .01 level. The number of cases turns out to be approximately 130. This is the size sample we would have to have in order to say with confidence that the experimental test *added anything* to the prediction of final achievement beyond what was possible from initial achievement and scholastic aptitude.

The example we have developed above uses one arbitrary set of figures. However, the figures are fairly realistic ones. The point that they make, and that would come out with any realistic set of figures, is that a study which is to add any dependable evidence to the re-

* A regression equation is a linear equation of the general form $ax_1 + bx_2 + cx_3 + d = \tilde{y}$ in which the values of a, b, and c are so chosen that the weighted combination of the three predictors x_1, x_2, and x_3 gives the most accurate general estimate of some criterion y.

** For this formula, see a standard statistics text, for example Walker & Lev [9], p. 337.

search literature on the prediction of achievement must be based on very substantial experimental groups, more substantial than has been typical of research on "over-" and "underachievement." And the more of achievement that we are already accounting for by known predictors, the larger our experimental groups must become if we are to establish the influence of further, more subtle, influences. Correlational studies of factors related to gain in achievement that are based on 100 cases or less will generally be a waste of effort.

PATTERNS OF STATISTICAL ANALYSIS

When we are working with a case of genuine prediction, there are two possible patterns of correlational analysis. We may compute a measure of gain in achievement for each person by subtracting his initial level of achievement from his final level and then correlate all our predictors with this measure of gain. Or we may calculate a predicted final achievement score, predicted from initial achievement and possibly also scholastic aptitude or one or more other variables, and deal with discrepancies between this predicted score and the obtained final score. We can then try to find other variables that will be correlated with this discrepancy—this "over-" or "underachievement." * The two approaches will ordinarily yield similar results, but they will not be exactly the same.

The approach that seems in many ways the most sensible is to deal with actual gain scores. After all, gains in achievement are what education is interested in, so from that point of view gains in achievement are what we should study. This approach works quite well as long as it is possible to express initial and final achievement on some meaningful equal-unit common scale, so that one may be subtracted from the other. When the criterion of achievement is performance on an objective test, and when parallel forms are available with scores expressed in comparable and equal units, typically some variety of standard score or grade equivalent,

* As indicated earlier, we could use the term "overprediction" just as appropriately as "underachievement."

subtraction seems an appropriate operation.* However, such crude gain scores are in several respects tricky measures to deal with. In the first place, crude gain is almost certain to be negatively correlated with initial achievement score. This is another manifestation of statistical regression. Since the correlation between initial score and final score is less than perfect, those who were highest to begin with will tend not to be highest at the end, and thus will show relatively modest gains (or sometimes actual losses in score), while those lowest to begin with will not generally be lowest on the final test, and will collectively show larger than average gains. Any measure that shows a higher correlation with the initial than with the final test will tend to show negative correlation with gains. Furthermore, if the test that is being used is limited at the upper end, so that able students may "hit the ceiling" of the test, and not have room to exhibit their full growth, this will also tend to produce negative correlation between predictor measures and gain.**

An illustration of the type of correlation that is found between scholastic aptitude and gain in achievement can be provided from some data collected by the author in 1960–61. The Lorge-Thorndike Intelligence Test and the STEP Reading Test were given in October to 4th and 5th grade pupils in several school systems. An alternate form of the STEP Reading Test was given the following May. The gain in STEP Reading, expressed in scaled score units, was calculated for each pupil. Correlations of Lorge-Thorndike raw scores with these gains were as follows:

| 4th Grade | + .087 | $N = 450$ |
| 5th Grade | − .124 | $N = 499$ |

Note that the correlations are quite small, and that the one for the 5th grade is negative. Inspection of the data indicates that a

* Even with the best of tests, the equality of the converted-score units is open to some question.

** The relationship of gain to initial score may be affected by various factors of a more substantial nature than simple statistical regression. Thus, if the teacher's efforts are focused on bringing the bottom half of the class "up to the norm," the top half may fail to make the progress of which they are capable, and the tendency to negative correlation between initial status and gain will be enhanced.

number of the abler 5th graders had near-perfect scores on the
initial test, and so had little opportunity to register gains, and this
probably accounts for the negative correlation. However, the main
point brought out by these data is that _gains_ in achievement are
predicted very poorly, even by a measure presumed to be assessing
scholastic aptitude.

Often, there is no common score scale in terms of which a gain
can be expressed. Thus, if we are dealing with teachers' marks in
English composition, for example, there is no meaningful unit
that can express the gain in skill represented by a "B" at the end
of the 10th grade followed by a "C" at the end of the 11th grade.
Even more clearly, there is no way of expressing the gain in
knowledge of biology for a pupil who received a grade of 85 in
9th grade General Science and a grade of 88 in 10th grade Biology.
Under these circumstances, all that it is sensible to do is to use
previous marks in a similar course or previous grade point average
as a predictor, possibly along with some aptitude measure. A prediction of final achievement can be made for each individual in
the group, and the discrepancy between actual and predicted
achievement can be calculated. Other variables can then be correlated with these residual or discrepancy scores. We can study
whether any of the other predictor variables are related to that part
of final achivement that cannot be predicted from the measure of
aptitude and/or achievement prior to the period of the investigation.*

PROBLEMS IN EXPRESSING RELATIONSHIPS

A complete representation of the relationship between two variables is given by the two-dimensional scatter-plot in which each
subject is plotted as a point that shows his score for both variable
X and variable Y. By inspection of this plot, one can note unusual

---

* Instead of actually computing a residual score for each individual and calcu-
lating correlations with this residual score, it is possible and usually computation-
ally more efficient to accomplish the same result by the statistical techniques of
part correlation. These are elaborated in Appendix B.

features of the distributions of the two variables, separately and jointly. However, a complete presentation of the data is never sufficient in itself for the research worker, so some summarization of the detail is necessary. The facts represented in a two-dimensional scatter-plot are usually summarized in a product-moment correlation coefficient. This coefficient provides an index of the degree of *linear* relationship between the continuous distributions of the two variables that are being studied. Problems in expressing the relationship between the two variables may arise either because (1) the relationship is not adequately represented by a straight line, or (2) one or both of the variables are not continuous. Neither of these constitutes a serious problem, and appropriate statistical techniques are available for dealing with each of them.

The possibility always exists that the relationship between two variables may be better represented by some mathematical function other than a straight line. Thus, average achievement in spelling may increase as IQ increases from 75 up to 110, but show relatively little further increase as IQ increases from 110 to 140. If the complete scatter-plot is available, it is easy to inspect the data for indications of such a nonlinear relationship. Well-established statistical techniques are available to establish whether any apparent nonlinearity is statistically significant. When a significantly nonlinear relationship has been discovered, it is possible to express the degree of this more complex relationship, and to transform the scores on the original variable in such a way that the new transformed variable *does* show a linear relationship. These matters are considered in more detail in Appendix C.

Indices of correlation have also been developed to express relationships of categorized to continuous variables and of categorized variables to each other. An example of a categorized variable that might conceivably be related to achievement is "mother works" vs. "mother is a housewife." If the relationship of this item of information to academic achievement is being studied, the two-dimensional scatter-plot collapses into two frequency distributions of achievement scores, one for children of working mothers and one for children of housewife mothers. The difference in average achievement for the two groups can be translated into terms comparable to the usual product-moment correlation through what is known as a point-biserial correlation. Other types of coefficients are available when both variables consist of discrete categories. There are further complications with some types of data, which we cannot go into here; but the main point is that data for almost any type of variable can be meaningfully expressed in correlational terms, so that different variables can be compared and the effect of combining variables in teams can be studied.

PROBLEMS IN INTERPRETING RELATIONSHIPS

Many of the problems of interpretation that we encounter arise when we try to eliminate the influence of one factor in a pattern of relationships to see what remaining influence is to be attributed to other factors. Most commonly, investigators have wished to remove the influence of IQ or scholastic aptitude, in order to study the residual relationship between achievement and other factors. A number of problems arise when this is attempted. We must examine some of them.

The fallacy of simple subtraction

One procedure for eliminating the influence of aptitude, which was used by many early investigators and is still found in current research literature, is simply to subtract aptitude score from achievement score and work with the differences. Of course, both scores must be expressed in some type of comparable units before they are subtracted, so typically they are converted into standard scores or percentiles. Thus, for a high school class of 11th graders, each pupil's aptitude test score might be converted into a percentile representing his standing in the class on the test and each pupil's end-of-year grades might be converted into a percentile representing his standing in the class on grade point average. The difference between the two percentiles might then be used by the investigator as an index of discrepancy between expected and actual achievement, and be correlated with other variables to see what the correlates of the achievement discrepancy were. This procedure is appealingly simple. Unfortunately it is wrong.

The difficulties can be brought out most clearly by considering the top pupil on the aptitude test. What kind of a discrepancy score will we get for him? Of course, it *can't* be positive. He is already at the very top on aptitude; he can't do any better on achievement. Unless he happens to be number one on both, the only direction he can go on achievement is down. In the same way, the number two man in 100 has 98 ways to go down, only one way to go up. Conversely, the bottom one in aptitude cannot be worse in achievement, and has 99 ways of being better. In general, those who are highest in aptitude will not be so high in achievement and those who are lowest in aptitude will not be as low in achievement. (The same will hold in reverse, and those who are highest in achievement will not be as high in aptitude.) Unless the correlation between the two sets of measures is perfect, and it cannot be if only because of the errors of measurement in each, this regression effect will occur. Thus, crude difference scores subtracting aptitude from achievement will *always* have a systematic bias. They will be predominantly negative for those high in aptitude, predominantly positive for those low in aptitude. They will be predominantly positive for those high in achievement, negative for those low in achievement.

The bias in simple difference scores of the sort that we have been describing will, unfortunately, influence the relationships of these difference scores with other variables. As we have pointed out, the simple difference scores will have a negative correlation (and often quite a substantial one) with level of aptitude. In consequence, they will tend to be negatively correlated with any other variable that is positively correlated with aptitude and positively correlated with any variable that is negatively correlated with aptitude. This kind of a simple difference measure is not adequate for any analytical study of how factors other than aptitude are related to achievement.

The same distortions that affect the simple difference apply equally to scores derived as simple ratios of achievement to aptitude, and in fact ratios are even less defensible on logical and statistical grounds. This is why the "Achievement Quotient" has rather completely disappeared from our educational scene.

Predicted achievement and discrepancy scores

If we cannot work with simple differences between aptitude and achievement measures, how then are we to study discrepancies between aptitude and achievement? The answer is that we must predict achievement from aptitude, on the basis of the known correlation between the aptitude measure and the achievement measure. The prediction equation, or regression equation (see page 12), tells us the average or typical achievement score for individuals at any given aptitude level. This predicted value is an unbiased estimate of achievement, and at any aptitude level positive and negative discrepancies between *predicted* and *actual* achievement are equally likely and the *average* difference is zero. That is, the residuals are uncorrelated with aptitude score.

We may now study the correlation of any other variable with that part of the achievement measure that is not predicted by, and consequently is independent of, the aptitude measure. Of course, as we have indicated in an earlier section, a fraction (sometimes a substantial fraction) of this residual will represent measurement error. But a fraction of it may represent genuine achievement not accounted for by those factors included in the aptitude test.

If we are going to work with residual scores, that is, the part of achievement that cannot already be predicted, it is always possible to work with what is left over when we use a *team* of predictors. We can base our prediction equation upon two or more scores that we have for the members of our group. The statistical procedures of multiple regression * enable us to set up the most efficient linear combination of scores to predict the achievement measure. It is then possible to study the residuals from this joint prediction to

* For an adequate treatment of these techniques, the reader must be referred to standard statistics texts, for example, Walker & Lev [9].

see if we can find anything that is related to achievement over and
beyond the relationship that is already incorporated in our team of
predictors.

In practice there is rarely any point in actually computing residual scores and working with them. What the statistician does is
compute the complete table of correlations among all the variables
that he is studying. Given the table of correlations, there are two
main ways of studying the complete pattern of relationships to
understand what elements contribute to the prediction of achievement and to what extent. One is to apply the techniques of part
and multiple correlation and regression. The other is to apply the
techniques of factor analysis. Part correlation undertakes to determine the extent to which each predictor variable makes a unique
contribution to the prediction of achievement, and multiple correlation undertakes to evaluate the level of prediction that is possible
from the whole team of predictors working together. Factor analysis
undertakes to analyze the whole pattern of interrelationships into
a limited number of hypothetical underlying factors, and thereby
to describe the factors entering into the achievement measure.

Moderator variables

All methods involving the analysis of a table of intercorrelations
are based on certain limiting assumptions. Basically, these are (1)
that the relationships are all linear, and (2) that the relationship
between any pair of variables, say X and Y, is the same at all values
of any other variable, say Z. By way of illustration, if the three
variables are education of parents, scholastic aptitude test score,
and average school grade, it is assumed that the relationship between either parental education or aptitude test score and grades
can be represented by a straight line. It is further assumed that at
each level of parental education the slope of the straight line
representing the relationship between aptitude and grades will be
the same. This means that if the rise in typical grade point average
is one point for each two points rise in aptitude test score for
children of eighth-grade-education parents, it will also be one point
for each two for college-educated parents.

The above assumptions do not necessarily correspond to the facts. It is possible that aptitude test scores and grades are more closely related for some subgroups than for others. For example, Grooms and Endler [3] reported that aptitude scores correlated with achievement .63 in a high-anxiety subgroup of 22 college students, but only .30 for the complete group of 91. And Hoyt and Norman [4] found a correlation of .62 between the Ohio State Psychological Examination and freshman grades at the University of Minnesota for 127 students with normal Minnesota Multiphasic personality profiles, while the correlation for 99 students showing "maladjusted" profiles was only .31. Thus, in these instances, the degree of relationship for two variables depended upon the value taken by a third. The third variable, whose value determines the nature of the relationship between two other variables, is sometimes spoken of as a *moderator variable.*

Unfortunately, to get data adequate to test whether some one of these complex relationships holds requires many more cases than are required to establish a simple linear relationship. In effect, if we hypothesize that the relationship between X and Y takes form A for certain values of Z and form B for other values of Z, we must have enough cases to verify the presence of relationship A for one subset of values, to verify relationship B for another subset of values, and to establish the range of values of variable Z for which each of these relationships holds. There is no simple way of stating how much sample size must be increased to provide adequate evidence upon one of these interacting relationships, but the increase is certainly very substantial. It should perhaps be noted in passing that the two studies referred to above gave results which appear in opposition to each other, and that neither of the findings has been confirmed in further independent studies.

Criterion heterogeneity

Attention should perhaps be directed to the previous discussion of criterion heterogeneity (see pages 15 ff.). If the final achievement score, grade point average for example, signifies different things for different persons, the results of efforts to predict it will be distorted. If the variations in the criterion are random, so far as the predictor variables are concerned, they will serve as error variance and water down all the correlations of predictors with that criterion score. This effect will reduce the sensitivity of the experiment, and still larger samples will be needed if significant relationships are to appear. Much more disturbing is the criterion heterogeneity that is related in some systematic way to one or another of the predictor variables. Thus, suppose having mechanical interests were related to taking "easy" courses in high school, e.g., shop courses instead of biology or geometry. One would then be likely to find that persons high on mechanical interest got higher marks than was predicted from their aptitude test scores or their junior high school marks. The high mechanical interest group would appear to be "overachievers," whereas the truth was that they had been measured with a different and shorter yardstick.

It is for this reason that it is important to scrutinize rather critically the criterion measure of achievement that we are using. If we find under this scrutiny that the criterion measure varies in systematic ways from person to person or group to group, we must try either to adjust for the differences that we have found or to carry out our analyses within smaller groups for which the criterion score has more nearly uniform meaning.

4

Design II-B: Concurrent Correlation

A third design that has been quite popular in studying the determinants of achievement is one in which measures are obtained for a number of variables, including one or more measures of achievement, and the interrelationships of the various measures are studied. The design we are considering now differs from Design II-A, discussed in the previous chapter, in that the present design does not exhibit a clear sequence in time. In the present design, all of the measures can be considered to have been obtained at more or less the same point of time, usually the present. The relationships among them can be studied, but no one can be considered antecedent to any other. Clearly, our understanding of sequences of causation is much less secure in such a design than in the design in which certain facts were known about each individual at the beginning of a period of learning and these antecedent facts were compared with the learning outcomes.

What can we find out from a study of the intercorrelations among a number of concurrent variables, at least one of which is a measure of academic achievement? Clearly, we can study the *correlates* of achievement. It should be equally clear that we *cannot* establish *causes* of achievement or lack of achievement. Any one of the correlates may be only a *symptom* of the same underlying cause or causes that produced the low achievement. Thus, we may very well find that the low achiever tends to express a dislike for school. Is he a low achiever because he dislikes school? Or does he dislike school because he is a low achiever? Or are low achievement and lack of enthusiasm both merely symptoms of some quite different common underlying factor? We can never be sure from the relationships themselves. A study of the interrelationships among a set of variables describes the patterning that exists, but tells us nothing directly about causation. However, a good description of the existing pattern of relationships is at least an important first step to understanding causes. Thus we need not disparage the concurrent correlational pattern as long as we remain acutely aware of its real limitations.

In the use of the concurrent correlational approach, most of the issues that we considered in relation to the preceding design arise again. They will not need further discussion. However, certain other issues are especially critical for the concurrent correlation design, and we shall now examine these.

THE PROBLEM OF EXCESSIVE OVERLAP OF "PREDICTORS" AND "CRITERION"

When we attempt to eliminate the influence of one predictor variable, such as scholastic aptitude, so that we may study the relationship of other variables to a criterion such as achievement, we face a basic problem of determining to what extent the aptitude test score may legitimately be thought of as a predictor of the achievement in which we are interested and to what extent it must be considered a *part* of that achievement. To be concrete, let us suppose that achievement is represented for us by the total reading score on the Metropolitan Achievement Test, Form A. At one slightly absurd extreme, we might undertake to "predict" this score from a substantially concurrent performance on the reading test of the Metropolitan Achievement Test, Form B. But this seems obviously absurd. By one definition of reliability, and the one that seems logically most defensible (i.e., alternate forms reliability), Form A and Form B scores differ *only* with respect to the error of measurement in each. Thus, the differences that we observe between the two scores can reflect nothing but the errors of measurement in each, and so no useful attempt can be made to study "underachievement" on Form A, when that "underachievement" is defined as the discrepancy of the obtained score from the score that was predicted from score on Form B. When we hold Form B score constant, we hold constant substantially everything in Form A but error. Whatever genuine underlying factors make for individual differences in Form A make for parallel differences in Form B. We have built into our predictor variable exactly what we propose to study in our criterion variable, so that when we hold the predictor variable constant, there is no criterion variable left to study.

In this Form A–Form B illustration we have tried to carry the situation to sufficiently extreme lengths so that the paradox into which we put ourselves becomes very clear. The "best" predictor is of no use to us, because it already contains within it all of that with which we aspire to deal in our criterion. We have left ourselves with nothing but error of measurement to study through whatever other experimental treatments or variables we use to investigate the phenomenon of achievement. But the same problem still remains, though to a lesser degree, when we use a somewhat different variable as a predictor. Suppose that our predictor had been the Lorge-Thorndike Intelligence Test, Verbal Series. Though this test is not called a reading test, it requires a certain amount of reading. And it certainly requires knowledge of the meanings of words. Approximately one fourth of its content is a vocabulary test, while approximately half the content of the Metropolitan Reading Test is a vocabulary test. Thus, these two tests overlap in part in their specific content. Clearly, so far as two different tests have essentially the same type of content, holding one constant holds constant whatever is real and significant in the other.

But the overlap between the Metropolitan Reading Test and the Lorge-Thorndike may stem not only from common content, but also from the common impact of life-experience factors. Thus, whatever makes Johnny a poor reader, be it lack of books in the home or emotional conflict with his parents, may also depress his performance on the intelligence test. One very specific overlapping factor is "test-wiseness," or special test-taking skills. Insofar as the predictor test has been influenced in the same way by whatever factors influence the criterion achievement score, any potentially significant variations in achievement will be held constant when the predictor is held constant. That is, we may overcontrol when we control on a variable which shares either specific content or specific background influences with the criterion or achievement measure.

But on the other hand, if we are to speak of individual differences in *potential* for achievement, this potential must be expressed in some variable that correlates fairly markedly with the achievement measure. It is only as the measure of potential is correlated with achievement, potentially correlated at least, that differences in the predictor signify an expectation of difference in the criterion.

We are, then, in something of a dilemma. We need a measure of potential that bears some substantial relationship to our index of achievement. However, the measure of potential should not include within itself any of the specific components of the achievement measure. Nor should it be elevated or depressed (i.e., biased) by any of the background factors which have elevated or depressed the achievement measure. When we define "underachievement" in terms of the discrepancy between an aptitude and an achievement measure, we do not know to what extent we have defeated ourselves at the very outset by using a controlling variable (aptitude) that already has in it too much of both the item content and the personal history that appear in the achievement measure.

Thus, the interpretation of concurrent correlational studies always presents problems. We must always scrutinize variables which show a high correlation with achievement, asking whether they do not overlap unduly with the criterion variable. We must always ask whether we have not overcontrolled on a closely related variable, and thereby removed from the picture those differences between pupils in which we are really interested.

To a lesser degree, the above argument also holds for Design II-A, which involves actual prediction over time. That is, an initial measure of either aptitude or achievement may incorporate so nearly the same material, and so much of the same life history, as the final criterion test that we have largely condemned ourselves to failure before we start if we wish to find *other* facts that will make any substantial addition to our appraisal of final level of achievement. We may need to study learning over a long period of time, or learning in a rather novel field, if there are to be any meaningful individual differences left to predict once we have eliminated the effect of initial level of achievement.

GENERATION OF HYPOTHESES
AND TESTING OF HYPOTHESES

It is an axiom of science that an hypothesis cannot be *tested* by use of the same set of data that led to the generation or discovery of that hypothesis. That is, if we happen upon a relationship in one set of data, we must verify that relationship in a new and independent set of data before we can accept it with any confidence. Thus, we may have collected 50 different kinds of background data about school pupils, hoping to find some facts that are associated with school achievement. Among the 50, perhaps 2 yield correlations with achievement that we would consider significant if we had been testing only those specific relationships. But we weren't testing those specific relationships; we were on a "hunting expedition" exploring a wide range of possible relationships. Therefore it is really essential that we verify the tentatively identified relationships in a new set of data before we offer them with any conviction to our professional colleagues.

Most research studies of discrepancies between predicted and actual achievement have been to a greater or lesser extent what we have just termed hunting expeditions. The investigator has been exploring a number of facts and factors, with no clear or explicit notion as to which one or two would turn out to be the significant ones. Often in such exploratory studies a few "statistically significant" relationships are found. But a certain percent of "statistically significant" values must be expected purely by chance. Thus, the chance of tossing 7 coins and having them all turn up "heads" is less than 1 in 100, i.e., is "significant at the .01 level." However, if we toss the coins 50 or 100 times, we should not be surprised to have them all turn up "heads" a couple of times during the series of tosses. Even the statistically rare event does occur—just by chance. When a few such "significant" results are found within a set of comparisons, they should be deemed quite tentative until they have been verified in a new, independent set of data. Unfortunately, it is all too rare to find the investigator repeating his study with a new set of cases to verify the suggested relationships before reporting them. Much of the inconsistency and confusion in educational research literature arises from premature publication of findings from exploratory studies without first subjecting those findings to verification.

The need for verification, for "cross-validation" of findings on a new sample, becomes even more acute when we are dealing with the more complex kinds of interaction that were discussed under the heading of moderator variables (pages 46–47). This is so because the number of possible patterns of relationship of predictor variables to achievement is increased enormously when complex interactions of the single variables are also examined. If the complex relationships are allowed to emerge *ad hoc* from the data, it will almost always be possible to find *some* way of combining the predictors that will work fairly well *for the specific sample*. But a relationship of this sort is essentially meaningless unless it is tested out independently in a new sample of cases and found to hold up there too.

The degree to which a cross-validation study is essential depends upon the state of our knowledge when we commence investigation of an area. If we bring to our study enough knowledge, based on previous research and theory, so that we can set out a limited number of specific hypotheses about the relationships that we are studying, then our initial investigation can be designed to test these specific hypotheses, and can be considered adequate to yield evidence upon them. If, on the other hand, we start an inquiry with only some notions as to a range of variables that might possibly relate to the criterion that we are trying to predict, then any relationships that do emerge in our data can at best be considered suggestive and must be verified in a cross-validating study before they can be considered established with any firmness. Unfortunately, knowledge and research designs do not fall clearly into the either-or pattern that we have suggested above, and there are many in-between situations which involve a somewhat more vague situation than the first and a somewhat more clearly defined one than the second. In these, the need for independent verification is real, but not so imperative as in the purely exploratory study.

5

Design II-C: Concurrent Comparison
of Contrasting Groups

The design for investigation that has been the most frequently used in studies of discrepancy between expected and actual achievement has been that of contrasting groups. Typically a group of "achievers" is defined and is compared with a group of "underachievers" with respect to one or more facts that can be found out about the members of each group. It is somewhat surprising that this pattern has been so popular, because it is in many ways less satisfactory than the other patterns that we have considered. But partly because the approach is so popular and partly because it does have important limitations, we must consider it in some detail.

RELATION OF CONTRASTING GROUPS
TO CORRELATIONAL METHODS

First, it is important for us to see the relationship between the method of contrasting groups and the concurrent correlational methods that we have just been considering. The point that we wish to bring out is that the comparison of contrasting groups, though much more limited in the information that it provides, is not essentially different from the correlational method.

Let us consider a concrete example to see how this is the case. Suppose we want to study the relationship between emotional adjustment and academic achievement. Assume for the present that we are willing to use a personality inventory score to give us a measure of emotional adjustment, and college freshman grade point average as a measure of academic achievement. One possibility would be to take the students who were in the top quarter on GPA and the students who were in the bottom quarter. Average score on the adjustment inventory could be obtained for each group, and any difference in the two average values could be tested to see if it was statistically significant. But we could just as well prepare a scatter-plot for the whole group, compute the correlation between adjustment score and GPA and determine whether the correlation was significantly different from zero.

If the relationship between GPA and adjustment can be expressed as a straight line, then the results from the correlational analysis and the comparison of extreme groups will be consistent. That is, if there is no significant correlation the extreme groups will show no significant difference, and if there *is* a significant correlation there will generally be a significant difference between the extreme groups. However, in certain marginal situations, a significant correlation may not be accompanied by significant group differences. This is due to the fact that in using the top and bottom quarters we have discarded the data for the middle half of our experimental sample, and that an analysis based only on the remaining half is less sensitive than one based upon the whole group. Thus, when the linear model applies to the data, use of contrasting groups leads generally to the same conclusions as a correlational analysis, but provides a less powerful method of analysis. There is one exception to this last statement, which we shall consider a little later.

How do correlational analysis and the use of contrasting groups compare when the relationship being studied is definitely *not* linear? Which gives more complete and useful information under these circumstances? Consider the illustration of emotional adjustment and grade point average that we used before. Suppose the actual fact was that both the highest and lowest on GPA showed somewhat poorer adjustment than the students who made up the middle half of the class. In this case, a study which compared the top with the bottom quarter would presumably show no difference, and similarly the linear correlation would be near zero. However, if we had the complete scatter-plot before us we could see the evidences of a nonlinear relationship, and if we computed the appropriate correlational statistic, called the "correlation ratio," we could determine whether the relationship met tests of statistical significance. Further analysis could be carried out to bring out the form of the nonlinear relationship. Thus, comparison of extreme groups can tell us only whether there is or is not a difference between the two segments of the scale that we happen to examine. But a complete scatter-plot and correlational analysis can show us the shape and extent of the relationship at all levels of the variables being studied. We then have much more information in terms of which to understand the nature of the relationship between these variables.

CONTRASTING GROUPS AND JOINT PREDICTION

A further limitation of the method of contrasting groups is that this method is very poorly adapted to studying the joint effect of two or more variables, or the net effect of one when the other is held constant. Suppose that we have an index of degree of "underachievement" for *each* member of a group and we wish to study variables X and Y to see to what extent they are related to "underachievement." If we approach the problem via a correlational analysis, we can get the correlation of X with the "underachievement" index and of Y with the "underachievement" index, and we can also get the correlation of X with Y. Given the three correlations, we can then determine how much of a correlation there is between the best combination of X and Y and "underachievement" (the multiple correlation), or we can find how much of a correlation there is of "underachievement" with either X or Y taken singly when the other is held constant (the part correlation).

If we limit our data-gathering to the extreme groups on the "overachievement" vs. "underachievement" dimension, this type of analysis becomes extremely awkward, if not impossible. We cannot get any satisfactory index of the correlation between X and Y if we are limited to two contrasting groups, and so we cannot judge to what extent X and Y are measuring overlapping factors. We are limited to whatever we find out about the variables taken singly, and cannot fit them into an interlocking system of data. For this reason, a study of contrasting groups gives a much less complete understanding of the factors interacting with achievement, or whatever our criterion variable may be.

ADVANTAGE OF CONTRASTING GROUPS

But are there *no* advantages in the method of contrasting groups that recommend it to us? How does it happen that the method has been so widely used?

One advantage can be recognized, and we believe that in reality there is only this one. The method can provide a more sensitive test of the existence of a relationship *per case completely tested* than does a correlational analysis of a complete, intact group. By taking cases at the extremes (assuming a linear relationship), we get cases in which any influence will have the maximum opportunity to show itself. We are, in effect, putting a magnifying glass upon the relationship that we are trying to discover. So two groups of 25 chosen as the top and bottom 10 per cent of a school class of 250 may bring out a statistically significant difference, even though the underlying correlation is quite modest—too small to be significant in a random sample of 50 cases. If the measure that we want to apply is very laborious and costly, so that we can afford to study fully only 50 cases, it may be advantageous to pick them from the extremes. However, we must be very clear that the information we get from testing this top and bottom 25 will be substantially less, and the sensitivity of an experiment considerably reduced, over what would be available to us if we had tested the *whole* class of 250 and analyzed the results by correlational methods.

The legitimate use of contrasting groups is, then, purely a matter of economics. When we have one relatively inexpensive measure and one very expensive measure—expensive in terms of time or money or the difficulty of inducing subjects to cooperate—it may be a sound strategy to identify extreme groups on the "cheap" variable and then test only these extreme groups on the "expensive" variable.* Under any other circumstances, it will prove more informative to test the larger intact group on both measures and study the relationships of the variables by correlational methods. Testing the intact group will not only provide a more accurate estimate of a simple linear relationship; it will also provide a picture of the shape of a nonlinear relationship if one exists.

PRECAUTIONS IN CONTRASTING GROUPS STUDIES

Let us assume that for practical reasons of economy we have decided to carry out our study by selecting extreme contrasting groups. What precautions must we observe if the results of the study are to be sound and interpretable? In large part these are the same precautions that we have spoken of in previous sections. They refer in part to the composition of the contrasting groups, in part to interpretation of differences that may be found between the groups on experimental variables.

Nature of groups to be compared

When contrasting groups have been used in order to study "underachievers," the contrasting group has sometimes consisted of the other extreme group, the so-called "overachievers" whose achievement is well above what would be predicted, and sometimes of the bulk of average achievers who are performing at about the predicted level. These two types of contrast have somewhat different advantages, present somewhat different types of problems, and permit somewhat different types of conclusions.

If we can safely think of "degree of achievement in relation to expected achievement" as a single continuous variable, differing

---

* If it were necessary to reduce the total number of cases fully tested by as much as one fourth (i.e., from 100 to 75), it would usually result in a more powerful analysis if the reduction were achieved by using extreme groups, and in this case the upper and lower fourths (i.e., 50 cases rather than 75) would provide the most powerful test. See Leonard S. Feldt, The use of extreme groups to test for the presence of a relationship, *Psychometrika*, 1961, *26*, 307–316.

in degree but not in kind, then use of the "overachiever" group may be expected to provide the maximum amount of information for the amount of data gathered. The sharp difference in achievement between the contrasting groups will make them more sensitive, case for case, to any genuine differences in related variables. Thus, this becomes an efficient experimental design.

However, for the results from such a contrast of extreme groups to be interpretable, we must assume that the "overachiever" differs only quantitatively—not qualitatively—from the "underachiever." That is, we must assume that the same kinds of factors are associated, though of course in opposite directions, with "over-" and "underachievement." If, for example, poor study habits are associated with "underachievement," we would assume that one of the correlates of "overachievement" must be exceptionally good study habits. If the "underachiever" is emotionally unstable we would have to assume that the "overachiever" is especially stable emotionally. But in truth the facts may be that achievement at a level lower than predicted and achievement at a level higher than predicted are qualitatively different, and not just different degrees of a common phenomenon. Thus, both "under-" and "overachievement" may be associated wtih emotional instability, though for different reasons, and we might find no difference between the two extreme groups though both differed from a group of average achievers. Insofar as "over-" and "underachievement" are qualitatively different phenomena, with different causes and correlates, the comparison of extreme groups may be ambiguous and confusing.

The comparison of "underachievers" with a group of average or normal achievers may be less efficient in bringing out differences between the two groups, but the differences that are established will be more clearly associated with "underachievement" per se. Insofar as our interest focuses upon the "underachiever," the strategy of using a group of average achievers as the contrasting group will be the safer one and the one leading to more clear-cut interpretations.

Homogeneity in the criterion

We must also re-emphasize the importance of a homogeneous criterion variable in terms of which to define the contrasting groups. If achievement is defined by grade point average, for example, and if the experimental population includes a mixture of engineering and agriculture students, those who turn out to be "achievers" are likely to be primarily agriculture students and those appearing as "underachievers" to be primarily engineering students. Heterogeneity in the criterion measure is likely to be a maximum when sharply contrasting groups are studied, and the two contrasting groups then do not really belong to a common population. Other differences between them are then likely to arise from this difference in the population from which they are drawn rather than from the experimental variable (i.e. "over-" vs. "underachievement") that we believe we are studying. Some analysis of our criterion variable, to determine whether it is homogeneous, may be desirable, following the procedures suggested on pages 15–18. Where the criterion is found to be heterogeneous, it will be desirable to select contrasting groups within subgroups, each of which represents a homogeneous segment of the total population so far as the criterion variable is concerned.

Method of defining discrepancy between expected and actual achievement

If the contrasting groups are groups of "underachievers" and of "achievers" or "overachievers," it is important that we use appropriate regression procedures for estimating discrepancy between expected and actual achievement. As noted earlier, the score on the basis of which contrasting groups have been set up has sometimes been a simple difference score, in which an aptitude percentile or standard score has been subtracted from an achievement percentile or standard score. We pointed out, in the section on correlational methods, that this introduces a systematic bias. Those highest on the aptitude measure will appear in the "underachiever" group, and those low on the aptitude measure will appear in the "overachiever" group. Thus, the two groups will tend to differ in level of aptitude. There will also be a concentration of errors of measurement of reverse sign in the two groups. The "underachievers" will tend to be those who were overmeasured in aptitude and undermeasured in achievement, while the "overachievers" will tend to be those who were undermeasured in aptitude and overmeasured in achievement.

The appropriate method for assigning individuals to the contrasting achievement groups is on the basis of difference between actual achievement and predicted achievement. A prediction of achievement can be made by a regression equation relating achievement to aptitude (and/or some other predictors that have been found to be related to achievement). The difference between actual achievement of the individual and predicted achievement based on the regression equation for the group can serve to identify extreme groups of individuals showing high and low achievement relative to expectation, and the discrepancy score by which these groups are defined will then be unrelated to achievement or to aptitude.

Interpretation of differences

The discussion about causation that we presented in relation to correlational analysis is equally applicable to studies based on contrasting groups. As we said earlier, the two methods are logically equivalent in the linear case; and it is just as true of group comparisons as it is of correlational analyses that the data show only correlates of the experimental variable (here discrepancy between predicted and actual achievement), and that these correlates cannot be identified as causes.

By the same token, the discussion of the need to separate hypothesis-generating from hypothesis-testing is also applicable to contrasting groups. Often, a group of "achievers" is compared with a group of "underachievers" on a whole host of variables, to try to find some that are associated with "underachievement." Typically, in such an exploratory investigation a few differences are found that, if taken singly, would meet standards of statistical significance. Again, typically these few significant differences are mixed in among a whole host of nonsignificant differences. Under these circumstances, if we are to have any confidence in the stability and genuineness of the differences that we have found, we must verify them in a new and different sample. The first sample generated certain hypotheses as to relationships; the second sample serves to test or cross-validate them.

We can recommend the use of contrasting groups only for those situations in which it is not economically or practically feasible to test a complete experimental population. Under these circumstances, if used with the precautions that we have suggested, the method may yield results of some value.

6

Check-List and Conclusion

A CHECK-LIST OF QUESTIONS

This section summarizes much of the discussion that has gone before by presenting a check-list of methodological questions that each
investigator should ask, and answer to his own satisfaction, before
he embarks upon a research that is to contribute to the literature on
"underachievement." These questions are in addition to the fundamental one of whether the hypothesis or factor that he proposes
to study is a genuinely promising one that can be expected to throw
some light on achievement.

General questions

1. Have I an appropriate procedure for determining expected
achievement?
>   *a.* Have I taken account of statistical regression?
>   *b.* Have I used the best *team* of predictors to establish ex-
>   pected achievement? Have I included aptitude? Initial
>   achievement? Other appropriate factors?

2. Do I have a criterion measure of achievement that has the
same meaning for all cases?
>   *a.* Have I procedures to check for criterion heterogeneity?
>   *b.* Have I a plan to deal with heterogeneity if it is found?

3. Am I aware of the effect of errors of measurement on my
study: (*a*) in reducing sensitivity? (*b*) in producing bias?

Further questions on studies involving experimental manipulation of variables

4. Can I describe my experimental treatment adequately?
   a. Have I identified the crucial elements of the treatment?
   b. Can I describe them fully?

5. Have I an adequate control group or control groups to be compared with the group given the experimental treatment or treatments?
   a. Are control groups equivalent on the critical background factors?
   b. Are they equivalent on motivational and other intangible differences?
   c. Is the possibility of capitalizing on measurement errors excluded?
   d. Can assignment to groups be on a truly random basis?

6. Can I get criterion data on *all* cases in each group, to avoid bias and selectivity?

Further questions on correlational studies

7. If I am using "change" or "discrepancy" scores, are these sufficiently reliable to justify correlational analysis?

8. Is there excessive overlap of content between predictor and the criterion being predicted?

9. Is my group large enough to yield interpretable results, in view of the unreliability of difference-scores?

10. Have I made provision to identify nonlinear or moderator relationships, if these exist?

11. Have I adequate provision to cross-validate any hypotheses that may emerge from my study?

Further questions on studies using contrasting groups

(These are in addition to those raised for correlational studies, all of which are also relevant to the contrasting groups design.)

12. Is there *really* any good reason for using contrasting groups rather than correlational methods based on the total sample?

13. Have I prevented measurement errors or other types of bias from distorting my comparison?

CONCLUDING STATEMENT

In this paper, an attempt has been made to sensitize the potential investigator to some of the problems that arise when one attempts to study the discrepancies between actual and predicted achievement—discrepancies to which the terms "underachievement" and "overachievement" have often been applied. The paper has been concerned primarily with the problems of hypothesis-testing rather than the problems of hypothesis-making. For this reason, the emphasis has been upon the adequacy of the data produced by different techniques of investigation—adequacy both in kind and in amount.

The causes of "underachievement" are in all probability manifold. Many of these causative factors may well represent contingencies that arise in only a minority of cases. The contingency, or complex of contingencies, may be quite important when it does occur, but occur so infrequently that its influence cannot be convincingly demonstrated by statistical studies. Intensive study of individual cases may generate a high level of intuitive confidence in the importance of some such factor in a specific case. How to verify and test such clinical insights is one of the chronic problems of psychological and educational research.

The verified factors will tend to be those that are widespread in their influence, playing some part in determining the achievement of many or most pupils. Researches on the determinants of "underachievement" have identified a few such factors. However, a distressingly large number of the factors that are suggested in one study fail to be confirmed in another. These failures are certainly due in part to deficiencies of experimental design of the sorts described in this paper. If these deficiencies are eliminated in future studies, it is to be hoped that we will have a richer yield of consistent and confirmed results.

Appendix A

Standard deviation of discrepancy score

The formula for the standard deviation of a discrepancy score is a well-known statistical formula, but is more commonly designated the "standard error of estimate." That is, it is the standard deviation of the "errors" made in estimating one variable, say C, from another, say P. But these "errors of estimation" are just what we have been talking about as "discrepancies," i.e., discrepancies between predicted and actual achievement. The formula, which will be found in standard statistics texts, is

Standard error of estimate
of y from x
$$S_{yx} = S_y\sqrt{1 - r_{xy}^2}$$

In the present context, in which we speak of the discrepancy between a criterion score (C) on an achievement measure and the predicted criterion score predicted from some aptitude or other predictor measure (P), the formula becomes

Standard deviation of
discrepancy score
$$S_D = S_C\sqrt{1 - r_{PC}^2}$$

Reliability of discrepancy score

The discrepancy between an obtained criterion score and a criterion score predicted from some other measure is given by

$$x_D = x_C - r_{PC} \frac{S_C}{S_P} x_P$$

where all x's represent deviations from the means of the respective distributions.

The correlation between two independent measures of the discrepancy, $r_{DD'}$, would be given by

$$r_{DD'} = \frac{1}{N} \frac{\Sigma x_D x_{D'}}{S_D S_{D'}} = \frac{1}{N} \frac{\Sigma \left(x_C - r_{PC} \frac{S_C}{S_P} x_P \right) \left(x_{C'} - r_{P'C'} \frac{S_{C'}}{S_{P'}} x_{P'} \right)}{S_C S_{C'} \sqrt{(1 - r_{PC}^2)(1 - r_{P'C'}^2)}}$$

If it is assumed that D and D', C and C', P and P' are parallel and equivalent measures, then $S_C = S_{C'}$, $S_P = S_{P'}$, $r_{PC} = r_{P'C'}$, and we have

$$r_{DD'} = \frac{\frac{1}{N}\left(\Sigma x_C x_{C'} - r_{PC} \frac{S_C}{S_P} \Sigma x_C x_{P'} - r_{PC} \frac{S_C}{S_P} \Sigma x_{C'} x_P + r_{PC}^2 \frac{S_C^2}{S_P^2} \Sigma x_P x_{P'} \right)}{S_C^2 (1 - r_{PC}^2)}$$

But

$$\frac{1}{N} \Sigma x_C x_{C'} = S_C S_{C'} r_{CC'}$$

$$\frac{1}{N} \Sigma x_C x_P = S_C S_P r_{CP}$$

$$\frac{1}{N} \Sigma x_P x_{P'} = S_P S_{P'} r_{PP'}$$

And so, by substitution in the previous formula, we get

$$r_{DD'} = \frac{S_C^2 r_{CC'} - S_C^2 r_{PC}^2 - S_C^2 r_{PC}^2 + S_C^2 r_{PC}^2 r_{PP'}}{S_C^2 (1 - r_{PC}^2)}$$

or

$$r_{DD'} = \frac{r_{CC'} - 2 r_{PC}^2 + r_{PC}^2 r_{PP'}}{1 - r_{PC}^2}$$

Rearranging terms, and substituting the simpler notation r_P for $r_{PP'}$, r_C for $r_{CC'}$, and r_D for $r_{DD'}$, we get

$$r_D = \frac{r_O + 2r_{PO}{}^2 r_P - 2r_{PO}{}^2}{1 - r_{PO}{}^2}$$

Since r_D is the correlation between two independent measures of the discrepancy between actual and predicted achievemnt, it is an estimate of the reliability of that discrepancy measure.

Standard deviation of discrepancies arising from errors of measurement

For any score or measure we can compute the standard error of measurement of that score. The standard error of measurement indicates the variability that would arise in repeated measurements of the same specimen, due solely to the "error of measurement" in the measurement procedure. The general formula for the standard error of measurement, which will be found in published treatments of reliability, is

$$S.E._{MEAS.} = S_x \sqrt{1 - r_x}$$

where S_x is the standard deviation of the variable in a sample, and r_x is the reliability coefficient for the variable for that same sample.

In our case, the variable that we are concerned with is the discrepancy score, D. If we substitute the values that we have previously established for S_D and r_D in the above equation, we get

$$S.E._{MEAS.\ of\ D} = \left(S_O \sqrt{1 - r_{PO}{}^2} \right) \left(\sqrt{1 - \frac{r_O + r_{PO}{}^2 r_P - 2r_{PO}{}^2}{1 - r_{PO}{}^2}} \right)$$

$$= \left(S_O \sqrt{1 - r_{PO}{}^2} \right) \frac{\sqrt{1 - r_{PO}{}^2 - r_O - r_{PO}{}^2 r_P + 2r_{PO}{}^2}}{\sqrt{1 - r_{PO}{}^2}}$$

$$= S_O \sqrt{1 + r_{PO}{}^2 - r_O - r_P r_{PO}{}^2}$$

This is the formula for the standard error of measurement of a discrepancy score, or in other words, for the variability in the discrepancy score that arises purely from errors of measurement.

Appendix B

NOTE ON PART CORRELATION

In the study of discrepancies between actual and predicted achievement, we are dealing with a set of discrepancies between actual final achievement and the level of achievement that would have been forecast on the basis of the known relationship between final achievement and some measure of aptitude or of initial achievement, or some combination of measures of both. We are then often interested in the relationship of some other variable to this residual or discrepancy. Thus, we might be interested in knowing whether socioeconomic status is related to that part of college freshman grade point average that cannot be predicted from knowledge of the CEEB Scholastic Aptitude Test.

The appropriate statistic to provide this information is the *part correlation*. This statistic accomplishes the equivalent of computing a discrepancy score for each individual, i.e., the discrepancy between his actual GPA and the one predicted on the basis of SAT score, and then correlating this discrepancy score with socioeconomic status. The formula for the illustrative example is

$$r_{(C \cdot P)S} = \frac{r_{CS} - r_{CP} r_{SP}}{\sqrt{1 - r_{CP}^2}}$$

where
$S =$ socioeconomic status,
$C =$ the criterion measure of GPA,
$P =$ the predictor, here the SAT, and
$r_{(C \cdot P)S} =$ the desired part correlation of socioeconomic status with the achievement discrepancy.

Thus, if the SAT correlated .50 with GPA, and if socioeconomic status correlated .20 with GPA and .30 with SAT, we would have

$$r_{(C \cdot P)S} = \frac{.20 - (.30)\,(.50)}{\sqrt{1 - (.50)^2}}$$

$$= \frac{.05}{\sqrt{.75}} = .055$$

Here, socioeconomic status will correlate .055 with the discrepancy between anticipated and actual achievement.

To state the matter more generally, we will change the subscripts and call

Variable *0* the criterion measure of final achievement,

Variable *1* the predictor, from which achievement is being forecast, and

Variable *2* the further variable that is under study.

Then we get

$$r_{(0 \cdot 1)2} = \frac{r_{02} - r_{01}r_{12}}{\sqrt{1 - r_{01}{}^2}} \tag{1}$$

This formula permits us to see how much relationship the variable we are studying has to that part of achievement that is unrelated to our original predictor measure—how much "over-" vs. "under-achievement" is related to this new variable.

Formula (1) applies when the prediction of achievement is based on only a single predictor variable. Analogous formulas are available for handling the case in which we are interested in studying the relationship of new variables to the residual discrepancies in achievement when our prediction of "expected achievement" is based upon two or more variables. The relationship of the multivariate to the single-variable case will be expressed verbally here, but for actual formulas and computing routines, the interested reader is referred to Du Bois' treatment,* especially Chapter 8.

---

* Philip H. Du Bois, *Multivariate correlational analysis* (New York: Harper & Bros., 1957).

In formula (1), the numerator corresponds to the covariance of Variable *2* with that part of Variable *0* that cannot be predicted from Variable *1*, i.e., the partial covariance. (All variables are considered to be expressed in standard score form.) The denominator corresponds to the variance in Variable *0* that remains after the variance predictable from Variable *1* is eliminated, i.e., the partial variance. Thus, the part correlation between variable *2* and the residue of Variable *0* that cannot be predicted from Variable *1* is the ratio of the partial covariance to the partial variance of *0*. That is,

$$\text{Part correlation } (0 \cdot 1)\, 2 = \frac{\text{Partial covariance } (0 \cdot 1)\, 2}{\text{Partial variance } (0 \cdot 1)}$$

In the same way, when more than one predictor variable has been used,

$$\text{Part correlation } (0 \cdot 1 \ldots k)\, (k+1) =$$
$$\frac{\text{Partial covariance } (0 \cdot 1 \ldots k)\ (k+1)}{\text{Partial variance } (0 \cdot 1 \ldots k)} \quad (2)$$

Here,

Variable *0* = the criterion measure of actual achievement,

Variables *1 . . . . k* = the variables that give a measure of predicted achievement, and

Variable *(k + 1)* = the further variable whose relationship to the unpredicted residual is being studied.

Routines for computing the partial covariances and partial variances are the same routines that are used in computing higher order partial and multiple correlations, and are described by Du Bois and in other standard statistics texts.

Appendix C

HANDLING NONLINEAR RELATIONSHIPS

The usual statistical techniques for studying relationships, and the prediction of one variable from another variable or variables, assume that the relationship between the two variables is linear. That is, it is assumed that for each point of change in the predictor variable, at whatever point on the score scale of that variable, there will be the same amount of change in mean score on the predicted variable. Thus, it is assumed that a shift from a Scholastic Aptitude Test score of 300 to one of 400 will be accompanied by the same change in expected Grade Point Average as will a change from 400 to 500 or from 500 to 600. When this is the case, the usual formula for the correlation coefficient applies. This may be written

$$r_{xy} = \frac{\Sigma XY - \frac{\Sigma X \Sigma Y}{N}}{\sqrt{\Sigma X^2 - \frac{(\Sigma X)^2}{N}} \ \sqrt{\Sigma Y^2 - \frac{(\Sigma Y)^2}{N}}}$$

In some cases, however, examination of the data will suggest that the relationship may not be adequately represented by a straight line—that the criterion or achievement variable may increase steadily over a certain range of a predictor variable, but beyond that range may increase more slowly or not at all, or even decrease.

Thus, the scatter-plot of points shown below represents a relationship that is fairly obviously nonlinear. As applied to this nonlinear

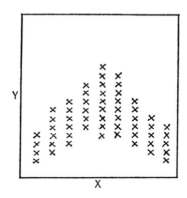

relationship, the notion of correlation becomes one of splitting up the variability of scores in Y into (1) the part that can be represented by changes in the mean value of Y as X changes—i.e., the variation in the means of the successive vertical slices in the diagram—and (2) the remainder, which represents the variation in Y within each slice. The variation of column means of Y is associated with, and presumably predictable from, X. The variation within the single columns is the unpredictable residual.

A correlation statistic, the correlation ratio (for which the Greek letter eta, η, is used as a symbol) expresses the ratio of variance in column means to total variance. The formula is

$$\eta = \sqrt{\frac{\Sigma N_j(\overline{Y}_j - \overline{Y})^2}{(N-1)\,S_y^2}}$$

where η = the correlation ratio,
   N_j = number of cases in the jth category on variable X,
   $\overline{Y}_j$ = mean of the cases in the jth category on variable X,
   $\overline{Y}$ = grand mean of variable Y, and
   S_y^2 = standard deviation of variable Y.

Since no relationship will ever be perfectly and exactly linear, the question that arises is whether the departure from linearity is statistically significant. This can be judged by seeing how much larger the correlation ratio is than the correlation coefficient, and testing the significance of this difference. Thus

$$(\eta^2 - r^2) \cdot \frac{N - k}{(1 - \eta^2)(k - 2)}$$

can be tested for significance by the standard F-test, entering the tables of the F-ratio with degrees of freedom $n_1 = k - 2$ and $n_2 = N - k$. In these formulas, N equals the number of cases and k equals the number of class-intervals into which the X variable is divided.

If the nonlinearity is found to be significant, the question then arises as to what kind of a function to use to express the relationship between X and Y. A natural approach to take is to fit a quadratic function, a second-degree polynomial, to the series of column means $(\overline{Y}_j)$. Thus, instead of having a linear function of the type

$$y = a + bx$$

we will have a quadratic function of the type

$$y = a + bx + cx^2$$

Discussions of curve-fitting in texts dealing with correlational analysis * will provide techniques for determining the best-fitting quadratic function, and for establishing whether the coefficient of the quadratic term is significantly different from zero.

Theoretical considerations may sometimes suggest that a function having some form other than quadratic be fitted to the column means. The general procedures for fitting an exponential, logarithmic, or other form of curve will be the same as those for fitting a polynomial, though details will differ, as will be seen in the suggested reference. In each case, the discrepancy scores that we will be concerned with will be between each individual's actual achievement and his predicted achievement, where the predicted achievement is the specified nonlinear function of the original predictor

---

* For example, Mordecai Ezekiel & Karl A. Fox, *Methods of correlation and regression analysis*, Third Edition (New York: Wiley, 1959).

variable. In essence, a new variable, call it W, is established where for each individual

$$W = f(X),$$

the function $f(X)$ being determined by the curve-fitting process. This new variable, W, may be combined with other variables to predict achievement just as the original variable, X, could have been.

The occurrence of meaningful nonlinear relationships is the exception, rather than the rule, in psychometric studies. However, one should always remain alert to the possibility and be prepared to deal with it if it occurs.

References

1. Diener, Charles L. Similarities and differences between overachieving and underachieving students. *Personnel & Guid. J.*, 1960, *38*, 396–400.
2. Frankel, Edward. Comparative study of achieving and underachieving high school boys of high intellectual ability. *J. educ. Res.*, 1960, *53*, 172–180.
3. Grooms, Robert R., & Endler, N. S. The effect of anxiety on academic achievement. *J. educ. Psychol.*, 1960, *51*, 299–304.
4. Hoyt, Donald, & Newman, Warren. Adjustment and academic predictability. *J. couns. Psychol.*, 1954, *1*, 96–9.
5. Kingston, Albert J., Jr., and George, Clay E. The effects of special reading training upon the development of college students' reading skills. *J. educ. Res.*, 1957, *50*, 471–5.
6. MacDonald, Arthur S. Influence of a college reading program on academic performance. *J. educ. Psychol.*, 1957, *48*, 171–81.
7. Mouly, George J., & Grant, V. F. Study of the growth to be expected of retarded readers. *J. educ. Res.*, 1956, *49*, 461–5.
8. Stamatakos, Louis C., & Shaffer, R. H. Effects of special attention upon potentially superior freshman students. *Personnel & Guidance J.*, 1959, *38*, 106–111.
9. Walker, Helen M., & Lev, Joseph, *Statistical Inference*. New York: Holt, Rinehart & Winston, 1953.